HOW TO SAVE HIGHER EDUCATION

William Griscom

ACKNOWLEDGEMENTS

This book resulted from the work and support of the board of trustees, administrators, faculty, and staff of Thaddeus Stevens College of Technology during my 23-year tenure. Much of the work contained in this book was performed by the Director of Assessment and Accountability, Ms. Cheryl Lutz, to whom I am indebted for all of her efforts over the years. However, the content and opinions expressed in this book are solely the responsibility of the author and no one else. My daughter, Sonja Helman, edited the book which significantly improved the original manuscript.

ABOUT THE AUTHOR

William Griscom has over 40 years of experience in higher education. His education began with a two-year technical certificate from a community college. He went on to earn his bachelors, two master's degrees and a doctorate in education. His career started as a public school teacher and upon completion of his doctorate he became an assistant professor of technical education at a mid-size public four-year college in 1976. He rose through the ranks to become a tenured full professor and held administrative positions progressing from assistant division chair to division chair (equivalent of a dean at other colleges) and special assistant to the president. In 1996 he was selected as the ninth president of Thaddeus Stevens College of Technology, a state-owned two-year postsecondary institution in Pennsylvania, where he served for 23 years, until his retirement in 2020. In addition to his higher education background Dr. Griscom was industry trained and certified to teach statistical process control, continuous improvement, and team problem solving. He did extensive consulting and training for such organizations as: Pratt & Whitney; Fairmont Specialties, a subsidiary of DuPont; and the Social Security Administration. During his tenure as president, with the direct support of the Board of Trustees and his team, he implemented the principles and concepts of performance based continuous improvement, which resulted in a total transformation of the institution into one of the best two-year colleges in America.

Dr. Griscom's experience in higher education covers a broad spectrum of certificate and degree programs from two-year community colleges to graduate level studies in a wide variety of positions. This coupled with his interaction with hundreds of elected officials and thousands of prospective students and their families, over four decades, provides him with a unique perspective from which to critique and provide recommendations on *How to Save Higher Education.*

PREFACE

In 1996 Thaddeus Stevens College of Technology (TSCT), a state-owned institution, was in serious financial trouble. It had been seriously under-funded for decades and operated in the red the previous year. As a consequence, its physical plant had deteriorated from deferred maintenance. Resources were so scarce that some faculty brought toilet tissue to work. Technical colleges require current technology to demonstrate and teach skills. Much of the technology the school used came from state and federal surplus, dating back to World War II. Dormitories had no air conditioning, television, or computer access and one pay phone per floor. Its progression and graduation rates were poor, especially for minorities. It failed its first attempt at national accreditation. At the state level there were discussions about closing the school or merging it with a nearby four-year state college.

By 2020 the College was widely recognized as one of the top two-year colleges in America, based on U.S. Department of Education data and national recognition by the Aspen Institute, among others. This was the result of high progression, graduation, and placement rates, especially for under-resourced and underrepresented students. The College added modern facilities with state-of-the-art equipment. It received bipartisan governmental support that provided a strong operating budget. The College had no debt and several million dollars in reserve. The median student loan debt of graduates was approximately $9,000. The College had over 1,400 employers offering over 4,000 jobs to the College's approximate 400 graduates.

This total transformation and the means by which it was achieved are unique in the higher education landscape. It is the direct result of the creation of a culture of evidence that uses objective actual performance data across every aspect of the institution, within a system of continuous improvement.

In contrast the majority of colleges and universities in America today are in crisis. Skyrocketing costs, high dropout rates, lack of actual learning, less available students, graduates who cannot get jobs at family sustaining salaries, and crushing student loan debt are all symptoms of the problem. Americans are increasingly questioning the value and return on investment of a college degree. Further evidence of the problem is the growing number of colleges and universities that are closing or consolidating: a number that will increase unless fundamental change occurs. Simply put, the current system of higher education is no longer sustainable. However, in an increasingly competitive global economy, it is vital to national security and economic prosperity that the country produce a significant number of qualified college graduates.

The root cause of the problem is the flawed basis upon which decisions are made regarding every aspect of higher education. This ranges from how students and parents select a college to how institutions of higher education are operated and funded. The solution to the problem is the widespread adoption of the system of continuous improvement that was implemented at TSCT and accounts for its metamorphosis. This consists of the identification of desired outcomes or key performance indicators (KPI's) derived from the mission. This is followed by the implementation of a data collection process that provides objective data across these outcomes within a system of continuous improvement. This approach can be attributed to Dr. Edward Demings who introduced it in Japan after World War II and is credited with the dramatic economic recovery of that country and its ascension as a manufacturing world leader. The system was copied in the United States and has become an integral part of management and leadership, ranging from manufacturing to health care. Unfortunately, with the exception of TSCT, it has not been applied in higher education.

In order to properly select, operate and evaluate a college certain data or information must be available for decision makers, whether it be prospective students and their parents, boards of trustees, accrediting bodies or state and federal elected officials. This data must be objective, complete, accurate, auditable, valid, span several years in order to reveal trends, and be consistent among institutions, to allow for comparisons and benchmarks. Below are examples of some of the most important KPI's that are available for TSCT and should be available for every higher education institution but are not.

- Percentage of students who graduate and get jobs in their field
- Median starting salaries
- Median student loan debt
- How much students actually learn, i.e., critical thinking, problem solving, technical skills, and general education during their time at the college as measured by national tests
- How long does it take students to complete their degree
- How satisfied are students with the education they received
- How satisfied are employers with graduates
- How have graduates progressed five years after graduation
- What is the success of different student demographics compared to each other and overall, i.e., males, females, gay, transgender students, African Americans, Hispanic, Asian, Native Americans, financially disadvantaged students
- Demographics of the student population
- Demographics of the faculty, staff, administration, board of trustees
- Cost per student
- Cost per graduate
- How do individual faculty perform relative to the knowledge and skills they are teaching overall and specific to all student demographics. For example, in a particular course how much do African American females learn compared to the overall class and compared to other student demographics.
- What is the success of various student demographics within specific programs such as Business Administration

How this and additional data are created and utilized will be covered in this book along with numerous examples. However, the book will begin by describing the problems with higher education as it exists today in America.

TABLE OF CONTENTS

CHAPTER 1
THE PROBLEM

Introduction to the Problem: The problems with higher education are numerous and complex, however, as with most problems there is a root cause and a solution that would resolve the most critical aspects of the problem. The solution and how to implement it is the subject of this book, however, first it is important to outline the scope of the problem.

The reason over ninety percent of students go to college is so they will be able to get a good job that compensates them well and will lead to a career that will provide them with a high standard of living and the ability to realize the American dream of home ownership, a nice car, the ability to take family vacations, disposable income and savings that will provide for retirement. Unfortunately, today a college education too often leads to significant student loan debt and skills that have no value in the marketplace, which condemns graduates to a life with little or no disposable income and a standard of living far below that of their parents. In many cases it has been characterized as little more than indentured servants working in jobs they hate and not utilizing the education they received.1 In short, the result of a college education is often the direct opposite of what was promised or desired. It must also be noted that approximately 40 percent of the students who start college do not graduate and consequently, for many, their prospects are even worse. 2 In addition to the personal tragedy this situation creates, it poses a serious threat to the long-term outlook of the economy. An economy driven in large part by production and consumption, both of which these graduates will play a small role due to their lack of marketable skills and financial resources.

This situation reflects the growing skepticism about a college degree as evidenced by the decreasing state support for higher education and the growing number of colleges which are in dire financial condition, resulting in a growing number of consolidations and closings.3 A number that will surely increase unless there is fundamental change.

The current general model of higher education consists of the following components: residential facilities and services; four-year programs of study; selective admissions; faculty tenure; board of trustees that represents the public served by the institution; research, intercollegiate athletics; liberal arts curricula; graduate schools; endowment to sustain growth; scholarships; and the granting of credentials.

This model can be traced back to Harvard, the first college in America. This model was copied and expanded upon as the number of colleges and universities in the country grew exponentially, until today there are approximately 5,000. This growth created competition for students, faculty, and funding. This resulted in a huge expansion of programs, facilities, staff, and amenities including such things as: tanning beds; extravagant student recreation centers; individual bathrooms; maid service; hot tubs; cafes and restaurants. This expansion increased dramatically over the last several decades in what has been termed an arms or amenities war in higher education. Over the last 50 years higher education took on more capital debt than any other sector of the economy including health care.4 Tuition from 1980 to 2010 increased by 1,120 percent.5 These dramatic increases in the cost of a college education made it necessary for most students to take out student loans, which also grew in size in accordance with the costs and have now topped the entire nation's credit card debt with 44.7 million borrowers owing over $1.7 trillion.6 It is not uncommon for students to leave college with student loan debt of over $30,000 with some over $100,000.7 Unfortunately, if they do graduate, they find there is a mismatch between the education they have received and the needs of the economy. Many programs produce graduates for which there are simply no jobs while many high-demand, high-paying jobs go unfilled.8 The graduates of these programs are faced with paying off their loans when they are unemployed or under-employed and end up living at home,

2

dependent upon their parents for a significant portion of their expenses. Their prospects for ever getting out of debt or owning a home and having a higher standard of living than their parents are very unlikely, or dependent on inheriting their parents' estate.

Cost:

Amenities: Numerous factors have led to the exponential rise in the cost of higher education. One of the most egregious is the ever-expanding list of amenities for the purpose of attracting students. The list of amenities is endless and includes individual residential rooms and private bathrooms. Some colleges offer what the students at Scranton University call maid service, which consists of a custodial member cleaning the room and bathroom on a regular basis. In addition, at Scranton University single rooms are available at a two-semester cost of $10,962 with the total annual cost for tuition, room, board and fees being $64,552.9 Louisiana State University in 2017 cut the ribbon on the lazy river where students ride inflatable tubes on a water current in the shape of the school's initials, as part of a recently opened $85 million recreation center funded by student fees. As the author of an article on this topic states, capital projects such as this are frequently paid for with 30 or 40-year bonds which places the financial burden on future students as well as current students.10 Below is a description of the recreation center of the University of Pennsylvania which ranks a lowly 33 out of 35 of the best college and university recreation centers in the country.

The University of Pennsylvania is home to one of the most luxurious fitness centers on the entire east coast. The David Pottruck Health and Fitness Center is a four-story facility that is complete with top-of-the-line fitness equipment, basketball courts, exercise studios, a climbing wall, and an Olympic-sized pool. Individual and group fitness courses are offered to students, which include activities such as dance, martial arts, and golf. Aqua fitness is also an available option that incorporates yoga, dance, and other cardio techniques with low impact water movements. Once your workout is complete, take advantage of a chair or a

3

table massage in the massage studio. As an additional bonus, The Energy Zone is located in the atrium of the Pottruck Health and Fitness Center. Here you can find fresh fruit, smoothies, energy drinks, and protein bars to fulfill your workout needs.11

Kevin McClure in analyzing the amenities arms race defined the following categories and examples:
Buildings: Recreation Center; Stadium; Residence Hall; Student Center
Free Services: Movie Theater and Snacks; Shuttle Service; Dietician; Coffee
Features Within Buildings: Multi-Person Hot Tub; Lazy River; Rock-Climbing Wall; Walk-In Closet
Food: Steakhouse; Major Fast-Food Restaurant; Roaming Ice Cream Truck; Lobster Dinner
Fee-Based Services: Laundry/Dry Cleaning; Art Rental; Ice Cream Shop; Tanning Bed
Technology: Biometric Scanner; Plasma Television; Online Streaming Services; Wi-Fi in Recreation Center 12

A significant problem created by amenities that are capital projects such as buildings and recreation centers is that they are funded for the most part, by long term bonds. These result in fixed costs that cannot be controlled or reduced during their lifetime, regardless of an institution's financial predicament. These types of decisions not only commit current students and administrators to these costs but future generations for decades. The impact of these amenities adds to the cost of higher education and as Manning states "has distracted the attention of students, faculty, staff and administrators from the fundamental purposes of higher education: the achievement of a high-quality education."13

Administrative Bloat:
Administrative Bloat or Glut is defined as the increase in spending on administrators.14 This increase has been occurring for several decades as indicated by the fact that between 1975 and 2005 while

the number of faculty in higher education grew 85 percent the number of administrators during this period grew by 240 percent.15 The titles of many administrators that comprise this increase did not exist thirty years ago, titles such as: Health Promotion Specialist; Coordinator of College Liaison; VP for Inclusion and Diversity; Title 9 Coordinator; VP for Student Success; Credential Specialist; Director of Active Learning; Dietetic Internship Director; and Coordinator of Immersion Experiences.16 Benjamin Ginsberg, in his book *The Fall of the Faculty: The Rise of the All-Administrative University and Why It Matters*, refers to many of the new positions as deanlets and deanalings all of which have staffs and assistants. Included in this growth are coaching and staff positions, for example, Kenyon College with 1700 students, employs 40 coaches in what the college refers to as "the best small-college sports center in the country." Other staff positions that seem questionable to most observers include coffee station barista and sushi chef. Much of the increase in administrators results in bureaucratic layering as exemplified by the leadership positions at the University of Maryland which has: six Vice Presidents; six Associate Vice Presidents; five Assistant Vice Presidents; six Assistants to the President; and six Assistants to the Vice Presidents.17 The situation is compounded by the high incidence of college and university presidents being overcompensated in relationship to faculty and abusing their power for personal gain. One of the most egregious examples of this abuse of power is the case of American University President Benjamin Ladner who resigned under pressure from the Board and was given a $3.75 million severance package, causing two board members to resign in protest. At the time Ladner's total annual compensation was over $880,750. He had requested the Board chair provide him with a package of bonuses and investments that would have added $5 million on top of his base salary over the next five years.18 An investigation by the Board of Trustees found among other things that Ladner had improperly used university funds for personal expenses including: a car and chauffeur; car for his wife; $6,000 in club dues; $54,000 in driver cost above the chauffeur; $220,000 in chef's services;

$44,000 for alcohol; and $100,000 in services from his social secretary.19 In 2017 over 60 college and university president's annual compensation was $1million or more with the highest being Bryant University President Ronald K. Machtley who made $6,283,616.20

Athletics:

Facilities

The justifications for athletic programs at colleges and universities often include the following: they provide the opportunity for students to learn critical career and life skills that cannot be learned in the classroom and laboratory; add to the institution's profile and result in increased enrollment; increase donations to the school; foster school spirit; and in the case of public institutions may increase state legislative support. The validity of these rationales varies from institution to institution but overall do not justify the cost to individual students and contribute significantly to student loan debt.21 Overall athletic programs are not self-supporting and require subsidies from the institution and student fees. Higher education institutions spend significantly more dollars per student athlete than they pay for non-athletes: typically, three to six times more. For example, in 2010 Football Bowl Subdivision (FBS) universities median expenditure per athlete was $92,000 while the median expenditure on non-athletes was $14,000.22 In 2018 the total of all three NCAA divisions' expenditures on athletics was $18.1 billion.23 Of that figure only $10.3 billion was revenue generated by athletics, consequently $6.5 billion came from institutional and governmental budgets, with $1.5 billion coming from student fees, which are commonly included in tuition bills but not itemized.24 A number of factors account for the exponential cost associated with athletic programs. Extravagant facilities are an important factor. Colleges spend fortunes on lavish athletic facilities. There is no better example of this "athletic arms race" than Clemson University which within the span of 18 months dedicated three athletic facilities which totaled $128 million. One of these facilities is the $55 million Allen N. Reeves Football Complex which opened in 2017.25 The complex was planned to be exclusively for athletes and includes: an 18 hole miniature golf course; putting green; bowling lanes; arcade games; barber shop; dining facility with two chefs and a nutritionist; lap pool; 60 person cold tub; nap room; golf simulator; basketball court; whiffle ball field; fire pits; barbecue; players' lounge; pool tables; turf softball field; locker rooms that are comparable to or exceed those of professional football teams; meeting rooms; amphitheater; 23,000 square foot state-of-the art weight and fitness room; and to top it off a metal slide at the back of the building if you would rather not walk down the steps from the second floor.

While Clemson's facility is one of the most egregious examples of the athletic facilities arms race it is by no means the only one. The competition for the best players out of high school continues to fuel this escalation in spending at all levels.

Coaches' Salaries:
The number and salaries of college and university coaches mirror the exponential increase in the cost of college athletics. In forty states the highest paid state employee is either the university head football or basketball coach.26 In 2017, 200 head football and basketball coaches made $1 million or more annually, while fifty of them made at least $3 million.27 An example of how coaches' salaries have dramatically increased is evidenced by the fact the first million-dollar contract was that of Bobby Bowden at Florida State in 1995. In the Southeast Conference (SEC) every football coach makes at least $3 million annually. At SEC school, Kentucky, the head basketball coach makes a salary of $9.3 million which is more than the total budget for any academic department in the College of Arts and Sciences. Additionally, the University budgets more annually for athletics than it does for undergraduate student aid. The annual salary of the Alabama head football coach of $8.9 million equals the combined salaries of approximately 60 of its full professors.28 The two coaching staffs (LSU, Clemson) that competed in the 2020 College Football Playoff National Championship made a combined $27 million. According to the Washington Post, the number of collegiate athletic teams has

continued to grow. In 2018 there were 63 more men's teams and 64 more women's teams than the year before.30 Consequently, the number of coaches continues to grow as does the cost. This is especially concerning when at the same time the number of full-time faculty is decreasing, and the number of adjunct faculty is increasing in an effort to reduce costs. *A History of Skyrocketing College Football Coach Salaries, from Camp to Dabo* by Richard Johnson documents the exponential growth in the compensation of college coaches from 1869 to the present.31 The cost of coaches is a significant factor in the increasing cost of higher education. When the head football coach makes five times more than the university president, clearly, there is an issue with priorities.

Reduced State Support:

A common explanation for the increased cost of college is reduced state and local funding for higher education. However, there is strong disagreement about this claim. This disagreement occurs even when opposing sides are citing the same data. For example, in an article in *Inside Higher Education*, the author describes how a conservative think tank and a progressive think tank reach completely different conclusions on this subject based on data found in the annual report of the State Higher Education Executive Officers Association. The conservative think tank concludes that inflation-adjusted state funding per student from 1980 to 2019 increased by almost $2,000. The progressive think tank concludes that overall state funding for public two and four-year colleges in the school year ending in 2018 was more than $6.6 billion below what it was in 2008.32 Regardless of whether state funding increased, stayed the same or declined, one thing for certain is that state funding relative to the total cost of education is less and tuition paid by students is more. State funding accounted for 79 percent of total universities' funding (state funding plus tuition) in 1980. By 2019 it accounted for 55 percent, which meant state funding shrunk dramatically as a source of funding.33 The difference was made up by increases in tuition which according to the U.S. Bureau of Labor Statistics were 1,416 percent higher in

2012 versus 1978.34 The level of state funding, while a factor, does not account for the exponential increase in the cost of tuition over the last three decades.

Changing Demographics:

While the world's population has continued to increase overall, the rate of increase has decreased. The highest was 2.09 percent in 1968. The rate of growth today is 1.03 percent and is projected to drop to .05 percent by 2050. This decline, in addition to a number of other factors in the United States, has resulted in a decline in the number of high school graduates and, consequently, the pool of students eligible to enroll in college. Over the next few years, the impact will be a loss of almost 15 percent of college-aged students. If the qualifications and ability to pay are factored in, the loss is even greater.

This trend is evident in a number of reports from the Western Interstate Commission for Higher Education whose Policy Analysis and Research unit offers various resources to support better informed decision-making, principally for 15 western states.35 In his book *Demographics and the Demand for Higher Education*, Nathan Grawe developed a Higher Education Demand Index (HEDI) based on data from the National Center for Educational Statistics', Education Longitudinal Study of 2002. His conclusion was that most of higher education institutions will be negatively impacted by the smaller pool of students available for enrollment.36 When these facts are coupled with growing skepticism about the value of a college education, unless significant changes are made that reduce costs and increase value, many colleges will not survive.

Drop-Out Rates/Graduation Rates:

The overall percentage of students who start college and do not graduate in the United States is 40 percent. Of the students enrolled, 57 percent take six years or more to graduate.37 There is significant variation in these statistics among private elite colleges, state-owned colleges and universities, and community colleges. There are also significant differences among first generation low-income and second-generation college students and within socioeconomic groups. However, the overall percentages represent a fundamental problem with higher education. Those students who do not graduate commonly have significant student loan debt but have not earned a credential and are much more likely to default on their student loans.38 For those students who graduate but not on time, adding two or more years of tuition and fees significantly increases their student loan debt. Of the students who do graduate, not finding a job in their field at a family sustaining salary compounds the problem. This topic is the subject of the next section.

Mismatch between Output of Higher Education and the Needs of the Workplace:

Thousands of college graduates are unemployed or underemployed while thousands of good jobs remain unfilled. The root cause of this problem is the lack of a rational career exploration system in our schools coupled with a lack of reliable information about the outcomes of college programs of study. America spends approximately $739 billion annually on K-12 education. Even when viewed as a percentage of GDP, this is significantly more than most nations. Ironically, very little of that funding goes to career exploration. Most adults find themselves in careers that were the result of serendipity rather than any rational process. It should come as no surprise that nearly two-thirds of college graduates have serious regrets about their education.39 For an example, every year American colleges and universities award 120,000 baccalaureate degrees in Criminal Justice.40 Consequently, 72.2% of these graduates report that they are unemployed or underemployed.41 When you couple this with the fact that Criminal Justice ranks seventh on the list of the worst college majors by median earnings, it is predictable that many of these graduates have regrets about their choice of a program of study.42 It also exemplifies the problem created by a lack of a rational and robust career exploration system. It is not a coincidence that some of the most popular television shows are:

NCIS; Criminal Minds; CSI: Crime Scene Investigation; Law & Order; Crossing the Line; Bones; Law & Order: Special Victims Unit; and NCIS: Los Angeles. While these shows portray careers in criminal justice in a very positive way, they are fictional representations that should not be used as the primary means of selecting a college major. If these students knew in advance: the number of students who started the program and actually graduated and how long it took; the median starting salary of graduates; the median student loan debt of these graduates; the percentage of graduates who got jobs in their field; and how satisfied graduates were with their education, it very doubtful many of them would have chosen Criminal Justice as a major. Another consequence of the absence of a rational career exploration component and students making uninformed career decisions, according to the National Center for Education Statistics, is that approximately 80 percent of students change their majors before they graduate.43 Among other consequences, this lengthens the time to graduation and adds to student loan debt. Traditionally college and career exploration were the responsibility of the school guidance counselor. However, with numerous other responsibilities and a national average of 424 students per counselor, little serious career exploration occurs. A rational system of career exploration should start early and expose students to a wide variety of career options. There are literally tens of thousands of different careers. Each has its own unique set of characteristics. In a rational career exploration system students would go through a thorough career assessment process that would help identify their personality type, skills, values, interests, and aptitudes. As children develop interest and aptitudes these should be documented and matched to the myriad career opportunities that exist in the world of work. This should include the various means available to gain the qualifications necessary to enter each career.

In the study, *The Permanent Detour: Underemployment's Long-Term Effect on the Careers of College Grads*, it was discovered that 43 percent of college graduates were underemployed in their first job. Furthermore, as these underemployed graduates

11

progressed, "the cycle of underemployment became progressively more difficult to escape."45 The consequence of these statistics is that a large number of students who go to college are unemployed or underemployed with significant student loan debt while at the same time jobs that offer family sustaining compensation and benefits go unfilled. This has been called the "skills gap" or the mismatch between the output of higher education and the needs of the economy. The best example of this mismatch can be seen in the manufacturing sector of the U.S. economy. Manufacturing is critical to the country's economy, accounting for approximately $2.2 trillion. The average annual salary and benefits of a manufacturing job is over $70,000 and manufacturing jobs account for ten percent of the workforce.46 However, a recent study by Deloitte and the Manufacturing Institute estimates that within nine years there will be 2.1 million unfilled jobs in this sector.47 It is paradoxical that a large number of college graduates who are underemployed or unemployed because the students took the wrong majors in college and do not have the skills required to obtain these jobs. A strong rational career exploration system would do much to correct this situation.

Lack of Real Learning/Value Added (Outcomes):
The high cost of a college degree has made it one of the most expensive investments a person will make in their lifetime. According to the University of Notre Dame's website, the full cost of attending for four years is $315,532.48 This is equivalent to purchasing a home. Considering the significance of this investment it would seem reasonable to have prior knowledge about the potential return on this investment. When purchasing a home most buyers do research on the house in question to determine comparable values. This also usually involves having an expert go over the property and identify all of the current and potential issues. However, when considering a program at a particular college or university it is impossible to find out even the most basic information, which renders making an informed decision impossible. It should be self-evident that one of the most important things a prospective student should know is how much they are

actually going to learn if they successfully complete a program of study. This can be established by testing students when they enter the program and then testing them again when they graduate. The school does not deserve credit for what the students knew when they entered the program but deserves credit for the knowledge and skills attained during their matriculation. A test that was developed for this purpose is the Collegiate Learning Assessment (CLA). It measures the core outcomes espoused by all of higher education i.e., critical thinking, analytical reasoning, problem solving, and writing. The test takes three hours and requires students to write three essays meant to evaluate their thinking ability. In their comprehensive book on the subject, *Academically Adrift*, 49 Arum and Roksa found that when the CLA was administered, at least 45 percent of students in the sample did not demonstrate any statistically significant improvement during the first two years of college. Further study has indicated that 36 percent of students did not show any significant improvement after four years. 50 It is also enlightening to know that of the schools using CLA they are only doing it for internal evaluation and on the condition of anonymity. This critical information is not available to prospective students, faculty, or boards of trustees. In addition to CLA there are a number of other nationally normed tests that measure other important outcomes of various college programs such as: Collegiate Assessment of Academic Proficiency; Collegiate Base; Collegiate Readiness Survey; Dublin Descriptors; ACT Work Keys; National Occupational Competency Testing Institute; etc. These should be administered at the beginning of the first year and just prior to graduation. The results, as well as information about progression rates, graduation rates, placement rates, student loan debt, starting salaries, graduate and employer satisfaction, and career progression should be disclosed to prospective students, boards of trustees, administrators, faculty, accrediting agencies, and the general public.

Increasing Compliance: Accreditation:

Higher education is one of the most regulated sectors of society and if recent events are any indication the amount of regulation will only increase in the years to come.52 These requirements account for an increasing burden on colleges and universities and at a questionable return on the investment. While there is a need for basic regulations in regard to safety, employment, discrimination, finance, and ethical behavior, the sheer quantity and complexity of the current regulations are overwhelming. In response to this increase in regulations the National Association of College and University Attorneys (NACUS) created the Higher Education Compliance Alliance (HECA) to provide colleges and universities a centralized repository of information and resources for compliance with federal laws and regulations. HECA created the Compliance Matrix which lists key federal laws and regulations governing colleges and universities. It includes a brief summary of each law, applicable reporting deadlines, and links to additional resources. The current matrix lists 294 topics. Many topics have several regulations. It must be emphasized that these are only federal laws and regulations with which colleges and universities must comply. Each state also has its own set of laws and regulations in addition to those at the federal level. For example, public higher education in Pennsylvania must comply with the Commonwealth's Right to Know Law.53 This law requires that a public higher education institution must provide the information requested by any citizen of the United States within five days of the request. Each institution is required to designate a Right to Know officer who is responsible for providing the requested information, with a few exceptions. For example, an organization in Florida would regularly request the names, salaries, rank, and service time of all the college's employees. They could also request the emails of any employee on a specific topic or between an employee and another person. By law, the college was required to provide this information and could only charge for the cost of copying. There are examples of former disgruntled employees at colleges using this law to harass the institutions by whom they had been employed, in order to create significant legal expenses and burdensome workloads. In addition, legislators will often make inquiries that require a response. Some of these requests require several days of staff time to fulfill and are already covered by other regulations. An example of such a request from Senator Bob Casey is included in Appendix 2. The cost of compliance is significant in terms of time and money. However, the cost of noncompliance is much worse in regard to fines, lawsuits, and reputation. Based on my experience the return on these requirements is minimal at best. It is incongruous with all of these laws and regulations, not to mention the amount of work required to maintain accreditation, an institution can be in complete compliance and fully accredited but fail to progress and graduate students with manageable student loan debt who get jobs in their fields at family sustaining incomes.

The Business of Student Loans:

Total student loan debt in the United States exceeds $1.7 trillion which makes it second only to the total of consumer mortgage debt.54 Over 44.7 million borrowers hold this debt. The average student loan debt of a four-year college graduate in 2016 was $37,102. Two million of the borrowers have over $100,000 of student loan debt and one-half million owe over $200,000.55 The Consumer Financial Protection Bureau (CFPB) estimates that one in four borrowers have defaulted or are delinquent on their repayments. The default rate of private student loan programs offered at for-profit schools is over 60 percent.56 Half of all borrowers are over thirty, 25 percent are over forty-five, and the fastest growing segment of the population with student loan debt is over sixty-five.57 The impact of student loan debt extends far beyond the individual and impacts the national economy both now and in the future. The current student loan crisis has the following economic impacts: slows the growth of new businesses; lowers rates of homeownership; makes it harder to weather a recession; suppresses consumer spending; delays traditional life milestones; reduces retirement savings; and shifts economic power away from students to lenders, investors, and colleges.58

15

The history of student loans in this country is well-documented and begins with the GI bill after World War II. The fundamental problem which is most responsible for today's student loan crisis was the shift from the federal government providing grants to students, to requiring students to take out loans. Colleges and universities saw this as a blank check and began raising tuition and fees for building projects and many of the other questionable expenditures such as amenities and administrative bloat that was previously discussed in this chapter. Clearly this shift in support to allow more individuals to enroll in higher education from federal and state grants, to individuals taking out loans, is a significant factor in the exponential increase in tuition and fees.

College Ranking Systems:

Selecting the correct college and program of study has never been more critical. The absence of vital information about the outcomes of programs of study, coupled with the substantial number of choices available at the over 5,000 colleges and universities in America, makes the process difficult if not impossible. The consequence of the wrong decision is reflected in the high unemployment rate of recent college graduates. Just as alarming is the 33.8 percent of college graduates who are underemployed, working in jobs that do not even require a college degree.60 In the absence of complete and accurate performance information about colleges and their programs, many turn to college ranking systems. By far the most notable among them is that of U.S. News and World Report, with over 10 million visitors on their website in 2011.61 The problem with this and other ranking systems is that with the exception of graduation rates, the rest of the data reported is not based on a college's or its programs' outcomes, i.e. employment in the field, starting salary, graduate satisfaction, employer satisfaction with the graduate, knowledge gained, or student loan debt. U.S. News and World Report rankings base a great deal of their calculations on inputs and factors which reflect an institution's wealth such as how much the faculty are paid or how much they spend per student. This coupled with other highly subjective criteria such as a college's reputation and peer assessment, illustrate how the ranking system's proxies for quality are inappropriate. The underlying problem with rating systems are that the outcomes data, critical for assessing the performance of an institution are not available. This can and must be changed. The later chapters of this book will illustrate how this has and can be accomplished.

CHAPTER 1 END NOTES

1. Walther, Matthew. College is Indentured Servitude. November 21, 2017. The Week. https://theweek.com/articles/738576/college-indentured-servitude

2. Collins, Michael L. and Joel Vargas. Why Millions of Americans Never Finish College. Bloomberg CityLab. February 27, 2017. https://www.bloomberg.com/news/articles/2017-02-27/why-millions-of-americans-never-finish-college

3. Higher Ed Dive Team. A Look at Trends in College Consolidation
Since 2016. July 29, 2021. https://highereddive.com/news/how-many-colleges-and-universities-have-closed-since-2016/

4. Rossi, A. (Director). (2014). Ivory Tower Is the Cost of College Worth It? Cable News Network. Note: In text reference is – Rossi, 2014, time in hours, minutes and seconds all in parenthesis i.e., (Rossi, 2014, 0:45:14)

5. Wittner, Lawrence. Today's College Students are Paying More for Less. History News Network, September 9, 2018. https://historynewsnetwork.org/article169899

6. Staff. A Look at the Shocking Student Loan Debt Statistics for 2021. Student LoanHero.January27,2021. https://studentloanhero.com/student-loan-debt-statistics

7.Berman, Jillian. Number of People Who Owe Over $100,000 in Student Loan Debt Has Quadrupled in 10 Years. Market Watch, April 8, 2017. https://www.marketwatch.com/story/number-of-people-who-owe-over-100000-in-student-debt-has-quadrupled-in-the-last-10-years-2017-04-03

8. Gross, Ashley, and Jon Marcus. High Paying Trade Jobs Sit Empty, While High School Grads Line Up for University. PBS All

Things Considered. April 25, 2018.
https://www.npr.org/sections/ed/2018/04/25/605092520/high-paying-trade-jobs-sit-empty-while-high-school-grads-line-up-for-university

9. University of Scranton Website – Residence Life.
https://www.onlinescranton.com

10. Riley, Naomi S. LSU's "Lazy River" and the Student-Fee Sham. Wall Street Journal, December 15, 2017.
 https://www.wsj.com/articles/lsus-lazy-river-and-the-student-fee-sham-1513381917

11. College Rank. The 35 Most Luxurious Student Recreation Centers, 2021. https://www.collegerank.net/features/best-student-recreation-centers/

12. McClure, Kevin. Examining The "Amenities Arms Race" in Higher Education: Shifting from Rhetoric to Research. College of Student Affairs Journal, Volume 37(2), pp 129-143. 2019

13. Manning, K. Organizational Theory In Higher Education. (2012). P.220. Routledge

14. Kaplan, Irv. Breaking Down Administrative Bloat. The College Post. April 24, 2019. https://thecollegepost.com/breaking-down-administrative-bloat

15. Berrett, Dan. The Fall of the Faculty. Inside Higher Education. July 14, 2011.
https://www.insidehighered.com/news/2011/07/14/fall-faculty

16. Hacker, Andrew and Claudia Dreifus. Administrative Glut. The New York Times. July 23, 2010.
https://www.nytimes.com/2010/07/25/education/25books-t.html

17. Ginsberg, Benjamin. Administrators Ate My Tuition. Washington Monthly. September/October 2011. https://washingtonmonthly.com/people/banjamin-ginsberg/

18.Jaffe, Harry. Ben Ladner's Years of Living Lavishly. Washingtonian. April 1, 2006. www.washingtonian.com/2006/04/01/ben-ladners-years-of-living-lavishly/

19. Ginsberg, Benjamin. Administrators Ate My Tuition. Washington Monthly. September/October 2011. https://washingtonmonthly.com/2011/08/28/administrators-ate-my-tuition/

20. Kamenetz, Anya. More College President's Join the Millionaires' Club. GBH News. December 13, 2017. https://www.wgbh.org/news/2017-12-13/more-college-presidents-join-the-millionaires-club

21. Peterson, Laurence. Is College Football an Expensive Luxury for Many. The James G. Martin Center for Academic Renewal. September 25, 2020. https://www.jamesgmartin.center/2020/09/is-college-football-an-expensive-luxury-for-many-universities/

22.Desrochers, Donna, M. Academic Spending Versus Athletic Spending: Who Wins? Delta Cost Project. January 2013. https://deltacostproject.org/sites/default/files/downloads/report/Academic-Spending-vs-Athletic-Spending-pdf

23. Baker, Kendall. Inside the World of College Sports Financing. Axios. March 11, 2020. https://www.axios.com/2020/03/11/college-sports-financing-student-tuition-costs

24. Lipford, Jody and Jerry Slice. The High but Hidden Cost of College Sports. The James G. Martin Center for Academic Renewal. December 24, 2015.

https://www.jamesgmartin.center/2015/12/the-high-but-hidden-cost-of-college-sports/

25.Brenner, Aaron. Athletics Arms Race How and Why Clemson is Spending More Than $128 Million on New Facilities. The Post and Courier. August 19, 2016.
https://www.postandcourier.com/sports/athletics-arms-race-how-and-why-clemson-is-spending-more-than-128-million-on-new/article_3c53d6c9-ec1d-5734-b936-9424ee7cc335.html

26. McKenna, Oliver. College Athletics Not Worth Cost to Universities. Daily Evergreen File. March 19, 2019.
https://dailyevergreen.com/47658/sports/college-athletics-not-worth-cost-to-universities/

27. Belzer, Jason. Making Sense of College Coaching Contract. Athletic Director U. June 18, 2017.
https://athleticdirectoru.com/articles/making-sense-of-college-coaching-contracts/

28. Nietzel, Michael T. Who Benefits From College? Coaches for Sure. Forbes. January 1, 2020.
https://www.forbes.com/sites/michaeltnietzel/2020/01/01/who-benefits-from-college-coaches-for-sure/?sh=249e584342e7

29. Daily News Editorial Board. Cash Football Playoff: Coaching Salaries in Clemson-LSU Title Match Highlight College Sports' Warped "Amateur" Culture. January 13, 2020.
https://www.nydailynews.com/2020/01/13/cash-football-playoff-coaching-salaries-in-clemson-lsu-title-match-highlight-college-sports-warped-amateur-culture/

30. Schwarb, Amy W. Number of NCAA College Athletes Reaches All-Time High. NCAA. October 10, 2018.
https://www.ncaa.org/news/2018/10/10/number-of-ncaa-college-athletes-reaches-all-time-high.aspx

31. Johnson, Richard. A History of Skyrocketing College Football Coach Salaries, from Camp to Dabo. Banner Society. August 15, 2019. www.bannersociety.com/2019/8/15/20732192/coach-salaries-history-highest

32. Seltzer, Rick. Dueling Conclusions on State Disinvestment. Inside Higher Education. October 24, 2019. https://www.insidehighered.com/news/2019/10/24/are-states-disinvesting-higher-education-it-depends-time-frame

33. Delisle, Jason and Andrew Gillen. Double-Check Those Shocking Statistics on State Funding for Higher Education. Real Clear Education. October 19, 2020. https://www.realcleareducation.com/articles/2020/10/19/double-check_those_shocking_statistics_on_state_funding_for_higher_education_110492.html

34. Editors. Cost of College Degree in U. S. Has Increased 1,120 Percent in 30 Years, Report Say. Huff Post. August 15, 2012. https://www.huffpost.com/entry/cost-of-college-degree-increase-12-fold-1120-percent-bloomberg_n_1783700

35. Seltzer, Rick. High School Graduates to Drop in Number and be Increasingly Diverse. Inside Higher Education. December 6, 2016. https://www.insidehighered.com/news/2016/12/06/high-school-graduates-drop-number-and-be-increasingly-diverse

36. Grawe, Nathan D. Demographics and the Demand for Higher Education. John Hopkins University Press. 2018.

37. Editors. Eye-Opening College Dropout Rates & Statistics 2021. Admissionsly. 2021 https://admissionsly.com/college-dropout-rates/

38. Editors. Eye-Opening College Dropout Rates & Statistics 2021. Admissionsly. 2021 https://admissionsly.com/college-dropout-rates/

39. Editors. 66% of US College Grads Regret Their Education, Study Finds. RT. June 26, 2019. https://www.rt.com/usa/462686-college-graduates-regret-education-deb/

40. Data Wheel. Criminal Justice & Corrections. Data USA - Deloitte. 2021. https://datausa.io/profile/cip/criminal-justice-corrections

41. Dufin, Erin. Underemployment Rate of U.S. College Graduates by Major 2020. Statista. July 29, 2020. https://www.statista.com/statistics/642226/underemployment-rate-of-us-college-graduates-by-major/

42. Marquit, Miranda. 15 Worse College Majors for Making Money. Student Loan Hero. November 24, 2020. https://studentloanhero.com/featured/worst-college-majors-money/

43. Editors. Eye-Opening College Dropout Rates & Statistics 2021. Admissionsly. 2021 https://admissionsly.com/college-dropout-rates/

45. Burning Glass Technologies and Strada Institute for the Future of Work (2018). "The Permanent Detour: Underemployment's Long-Term Effects on the Careers of College Grads" https://www.burning-glass.com/wp-content/uploads/permanent_detour_underemployment_report.pdf

44. . Editors. Eye-Opening College Dropout Rates & Statistics 2021. Admissionsly. 2021 https://admissionsly.com/college-dropout-rates/

46. Rector, Emily. Why Manufacturing Jobs are so Good for the Economy, and the Employee. November 1, 2018. Market Scale. https://marketscale.com/industries/aec/why-manufacturing-jobs-are-so-good-for-the economy-and-the-employee/

47. Zwick, Dillon. The Age of Disruption Part 1: I'm Getting Too Old for This Shit. September 7, 2021. Linkin. https://www.linkedin.com/pulse/age-disruption-part-1-im-getting-too-old-shit-dillon-zwick

48. University of Notre Dame Website. https://financialaid.nd.edu/how-aid-works/cost-of-attendance/

49. Arum, Richard and Josipa Roska. Academically Adrift. 2011. University of Chicago Press. https://press.uchicago.edu/ucp/books/book/chicago/A/bo10327226.html

50. Arum, Richard and Josipa Roska. Are Undergraduates Actually Learning Anything? The Chronicle of Higher Education. January 18, 2011. https://talk.collegeconfidential.com/t/chronicle-are-undergraduates-actually-learning-anything/

51. Higher Education Compliance Alliance. https://www.higheredcompliance.org

52. Editors. Higher Education Struggles to Meet Compliance Standards. July 22,2020. https://www.boardeffect.com/blog/compliance-higher-education-what-boards-role/

53. Right to Know Law. www.soab.pa.gov/FortheCommunity/RightToKnowLaw/Pages/default.aspx#

54. Whistle, Wesley. What is Driving the $1.5 Trillion Student Debt Crisis? September 1, 2020. Forbes. https://www.forbes.com/sites/wesleywhistle/2020/09/01/what-drives-the-15-trillion-student-debt-crisis/?sh=2c05dafe7aec

55. United States Chamber of Commerce. September 10, 2021. https://www.chamberofcommerce.org/student-loan-statistics/

56. Editors. Student Loans: The Problem. January 3, 2019. Center for Responsible Lending.
www.responsiblelending.org/issues/student-loans/student-loans-problem

57. Kirkham, Elyssa. How Does Student Debt Affect the Economy? Experts Weigh In. June 28, 2021. Student Loan Hero.
https://studentloanhero.com/featured/effects-of-student-loan-debt-us-economy/

58. Kirkham, Elyssa. How Does Student Debt Affect the Economy? Experts Weigh In. June 28, 2021. Student Loan Hero.
https://studentloanhero.com/featured/effects-of-student-loan-debt-us-economy/

59. United States Chamber of Commerce. September 10, 2021.
https://www.chamberofcommerce.org/student-loan-statistics/

60. Redden, Elizabeth. 41% of Recent Grads Work in Jobs Not Requiring a Degree. February 18, 2020. Inside Higher Education
https://www.insidehighered.com/quicktakes/2020/02/18/41-recent-grads-work-jobs-not-requiring-degree

61. Gladwell, Malcolm. The Order of Things What College Rankings Really Tell Us. February 2, 2011. The New Yorker.
https://www.newyorker.com/magazine/2011/02/14/the-order-of-things

CHAPTER 2
HOW TO IDENTIFY WHAT IS IMPORTANT AND PRESENT KEY PERFORMANCE DATA

Determining What is Important:

As President of TSCT I was responsible for leading and managing the College to ensure it was fulfilling its mission. In addition, I needed an objective measurable means of reporting my success or failure, regarding this critical responsibility, to the Board of Trustees. In order to do this, I needed Key Performance Indicator's (KPI) that were directly derived from the mission for each department of the College. This is a complex task due to the dozens of departments whose diverse range of activities includes custodial operations, athletics, residence life, security, financial affairs, academics, governmental affairs, health services, admissions, fundraising, and community relations, among others. This was accomplished with a series of meetings with every department to discuss the mission and how each contributed to it. From these collaborative meetings, KPI's were identified, and the current level of performance was used as a benchmark against which to measure future performance.

Higher education is comprised of a wide variety of institutions from community colleges to private universities. They are differentiated from each other by their unique missions. However, regardless of their mission, certain basic outcomes are expected from any college such as a reasonable graduation rate, the acquisition of knowledge and skills, employment after graduation, graduate satisfaction with their education, and progression in their career over time. Thaddeus Stevens College of Technology is a state-owned two-year technical college whose mission is *to educate Pennsylvania's economically and socially disadvantaged as well as other qualified students for skilled employment in a diverse, ever-changing workforce and for full effective participation as citizens.*

27

An example of a KPI, derived from the mission for the admissions department, was the number and percentage of financially disadvantaged students being admitted to the College each year. These students were referred to as "Stevens' Grant Students" because all students who qualified for a federal Pell Grant were provided with their room, board, tuition, books, and tools by the College and only responsible for the Estimated Family Contribution (EFC) as calculated by the Free Application for Federal Student Aid (FAFSA). Their cost could be as low as $0 for a student living in poverty or as high as $5,000 for a student coming from a better economic situation. The College also admitted tuition paying students.

In collaboration with the admissions department and input from the board of trustees and numerous other stakeholders, it was determined for the College to fulfill its mission that at least one-half of the total enrollment must be Stevens' Grant students with a goal of 70 percent. Therefore, a KPI of at least 50 percent Stevens' Grant students was established for the College and became the responsibility of the admissions department. This KPI's current value was calculated for every program as well as for the College overall. How this data was presented and acted upon to improve performance will be described and illustrated later. The process that was utilized to identify the KPI for the percentage of Stevens' Grant students was repeated within the admissions department for a number of other important outcomes. Another example of this process was establishing KPI's for the business office. One of the KPI's was to have no material findings on the annual independent financial audit. Another was that all vendors would be paid in 30 days or less. KPI's for all departments were created the same way and resulted in a total of over one thousand KPI's across the College.

Sources of Data or Where Do You Get the Data:
KPI's are data points. There are different types of data and varied means of collecting it. Below are the sources from which data were obtained for TSCT's KPI's and include the College's information

portal, surveys, national tests, and internal measures established and maintained by the College.

Portal:

Colleges employ portals today which serve as flexible, broad computer-based data platforms. They range from student information systems, handling applications and financial aid, to being used for online learning, advancement, advising, and other functions of a college. They allow for the creation of customized reports drawn from the vast array of data they contain, to provide specific KPI's. Their effectiveness is dependent upon the inclusion of all potential criteria that may be needed in the future during the data input stage. For example, if high school students' attendance is not requested as part of the application process and is not part of the portal's database, it is not possible to query the system regarding this factor. This was a criterion collected at TSCT and enabled the College to determine that strong high school attendance had the highest correlation as a predictor of a student graduating from TSCT.

Surveys and Questionnaires:

Surveys and questionnaires are used to collect data from a targeted group of people about their opinions, behavior, or knowledge. TSCT utilized the following surveys and questionnaires to collect data:

- **Graduate Satisfaction Survey** – Surveyed graduates about their satisfaction with the education they received after starting their first job following graduation as well as their starting salary.
- **Employer Satisfaction Survey** – Surveyed employers of graduates regarding their satisfaction with the graduate in terms of preparation, workplace skills, and in comparison to graduates of other institutions.
- **Five Year Graduate Follow-up Survey** – Surveyed graduates five years after graduation regarding their career progression and rating of the education they received from TSCT.
- **Student Satisfaction Questionnaire** – Utilized to obtain student feedback regarding satisfaction with: each faculty

member, course, and program; career services; athletics; dining services; academic support; counseling; admissions; learning resources center; tutoring; advising; technology; residence life; custodial services; extracurricular activities; diversity, inclusion, and equity; and other areas of the College.

- **Incoming Student Questionnaire** – Following acceptance to the College, incoming students were asked a number of questions regarding their plans and expectations. Questions included how many hours they expected to study, if they intended to hold a job, and if so, how many hours they planned on working. The purpose of the questionnaire was to identify risks based on the College's experience with previous students and then reach out to them in advance to counsel and maximize their chances for success.

National Standardized Tests:

There are two types of national standardized tests: norm-referenced and criterion-referenced. Norm-referenced tests compare one student's performance to others in a predetermined peer group. Criterion-referenced tests are used to learn different things about a student's progress. Some tests are a combination of both. All of the national standardized tests used by TSCT were a combination of both. The College administered these tests to students at the beginning of their first semester and again at the end of their last semester. The College took no credit for what students knew when they started the program, but the knowledge gained during the students' two-years of attendance was documented and reported as "value-added" by the College.

- **National Occupational Competency Testing Institute Tests (NOCTI)** – These standardized tests cover a wide range of technical fields. The tests employed by the College measure a student's competency compared to the level of skills and knowledge expected for a graduate of a two-year postsecondary college in a particular field. These tests are available for most of TSCT's programs. For example, the Computer Network and Systems Administration program's NOCTI test covered knowledge and problem-solving skills

30

for the following areas of the field: PC Principles; Network Connections; Physical Connection Types; Network Standards and Devices; Network Troubleshooting; Routing and Switching; Network Terminology; Network Architecture; Security; and Network Planning and Design.

- **National Automotive Technicians Education Foundation (NATEF)** – Appropriate NOCTI tests for the College's Automotive and Collison Repair programs were not considered appropriate by the programs' Industry Advisory Committees. It was determined that a better measure of the programs' outcomes were the corresponding tests given by NATEF.
- **Educational Testing Service (ETS)** -ETS is the world's largest private nonprofit educational testing and assessment organization. ETS develops various standardized tests primarily in the United States for K–12 and higher education. The ETS Proficiency Profile is a general education outcomes assessment of core skills —reading, writing, critical thinking, and mathematics — in a single test. TSCT utilized the test to measure gains in all of the core areas.

Internal Measures:

Internal Measures are the assessments, both written and performance-based, that are created by departments at the College. These internal measures are tailored to each individual course and by program. The purpose is to measure how much each student has learned and what percentage of the students are successful. This information is available for each individual student as well as by the demographics of race, gender, and financial status. These results are also utilized as an indicator of instructor effectiveness.

Data Integrity:

Ensuring that data is valid, reliable, consistent, complete, auditable, and spans timeframes long enough to disclose trends is critical for a performance-based system to work. TSCT determined that five-year time periods were the most useful for identifying trends. It was also determined that for the most part medians were more useful than averages. For example, when looking at graduates' student loan debt, the median was less affected by outliers than the average.

Maintaining consistency of what is being measured is critical in order to discover trends. If variables are introduced in the data collection phase, they must be noted and taken into account. It was also determined that response rates on surveys and questionnaires must meet a minimum threshold of 70 percent. For example, on the Graduate Satisfaction Survey, the responses of the first 20 percent were significantly more positive than the responses of the last 20 percent of responders.

Presentation of the Data - Dashboards:

In order for KPI's to be utilized effectively the data must be easy to interpret. This is best achieved by combining various kinds of data together in a form that is easy to understand and focused on a specific metric or outcome. The most widely used means of achieving this is the use of dashboards. This section will deal with how the data is presented using dashboards. The KPI's which I believe are the most critical indictors of fulfillment of the College's mission are:

- Enrollment (Important in the sense that the College was providing opportunity for the maximum number of students its capacity would allow. However, it is not as important as graduation rate which when coupled with placement rate is the real bottom line.)
- Progression from the first year to the second year (Retention)
- Graduation rate (Overall and by Student Demographic)
- Value-Added (Knowledge & Skills Acquired at TSCT)
- Placement rate in the field of study
- Median starting salary
- Median student loan debt
- Graduate satisfaction
- Employer satisfaction

Each KPI is composed of a number of subordinate KPI's. For example, enrollment has numerous components that include male, female, LGBQ+, African American, Asian, Hispanic, Native American, Stevens' Grant Student, and Tuition Paying Student. Since they impact the mission and the overall enrollment of the College it is critical to monitor all of these groups. This is most efficiently done by a dashboard that shows the current enrollment of each group and also the enrollment over a minimum of a five-year period. In the first dashboard below, overall enrollment is shown for a ten-year period. The second dashboard breaks down first-year enrollment over the same time period by the subordinate groups that comprise it.

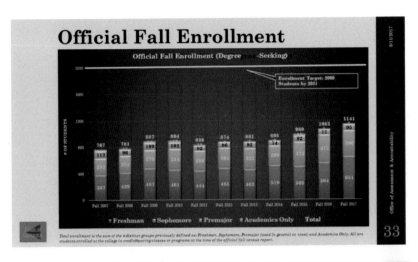

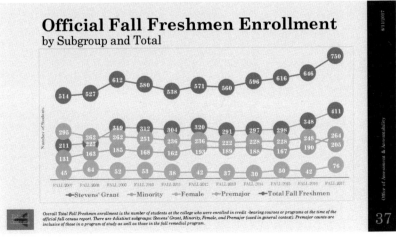

Additional dashboards were categorized by these subordinate groups for each program at the College. These dashboards made it easy to see which programs were successfully contributing to the College's overall enrollment as well as its commitment to diversity and equity in regard to the students it was enrolling. How this information was used to increase overall enrollment and better fulfill the College's mission will be the topic of the last chapter of this book.

CHAPTER 3

INTERPRETING AND UNPACKING THE DATA: A DATA DRIVEN DIALOG

Data Bias:

The best way to utilize the data which has been collected and organized into dashboards is through an ongoing dialog with all of the individuals associated with the data (KPI) or who have a role in the outcome it measures. Before discussing the data, it is important for all individuals involved to suspend their preconceived ideas and to replace hunches and feelings with data-based facts, in order to examine patterns and trends of KPI's that generate root-cause discussions. This moves the process from identifying symptoms to implementing changes with the potential to improve performance. A simple way to do this is to have all participants individually disclose their assumptions and predictions regarding each KPI. For example, faculty in a program may assume student failure is due to students being admitted to the program that are not academically qualified. This assumption should be set aside until evidence of the students' academic qualifications are presented. Employing this practice prior to engaging in the data driven dialog helps mitigate data bias which compromises the process.

Structured Data Driven Dialog:

The outcome of an effective data driven dialog is an interpretation of the data that leads to actions that have the potential to improve performance. The first step is to assemble the KPI's in the form of a data driven dialog sheet that relates the KPI's to the College's mission and includes data spanning at least five years. Below is an example of a data driven dialog sheet template that was used for every program at TSCT. The 16 questions are designed to assess every aspect of the program as it relates to the College's mission and performance. Metrics of Success are the KPI's related to each question. Program Performance Metric is the actual performance of the program under review relative to the specific KPI. Benchmarks are the individual program's performance compared to the College's overall performance or the College's goal for a particular KPI. Data Source/Location discloses the source from which the data was obtained; this is often taken directly from the program's dashboards which are continually updated and published. Data Person Responsible is the person(s) who will be responsible for obtaining the data and ensuring its accuracy.

*Less than 5-year Performance Metric

1. Is this program contributing to the fulfillment of our mission?

Metric of Success [KPI]	Program Performance Metric	Benchmark (NA = Not Applicable)	Data Source/Location	Data Person Responsible
Enrollment [1A]	Enrollment Trends	Program Capacity	Program Dashboard	
Diversity – Stevens' Grant [11A]	Enrollment Trends	70% Enrollment Target	Program Dashboard	
Diversity – Minority [12A]	Enrollment Trends	30% Enrollment Target	Program Dashboard	
Diversity – Female [13A]	Enrollment Trends	20% Enrollment Target	Program Dashboard	
Diversity – Premajor (in a POS) [14A]	Enrollment Trends	10% or Less Enrollment Target	Program Dashboard	

Employment Demand [6B]	Average # of Jobs per Program/Graduate Trends	5-Year TSCT Median	Program/Institutional Dashboard
Family Sustainable Wage [8]	Graduate Annual Starting Salary Trends	5-Year TSCT Median	Program Dashboard
Student Loan Debt [10]	*5-Year Median Loan Debt	5-Year TSCT Median	Program/Institutional Dashboard

2. Are students succeeding in this program? (success defined as graduation within normal time and employed fulltime in major, within 1 year of graduation)

Metric of Success [KPI]	Program Performance Metric	Benchmark (NA = Not Applicable)	Source/Location	Person Responsible
Progression Rate [2]	5-Year Trends	10-Year TSCT Median	Program Dashboard	
Graduation Rate [2]	5-Year Trends	10-Year TSCT Median	Program Dashboard	
% Graduates Employed Fulltime in Major (Response Rate) [6B & 6A]	5-Year Trends	5-Year TSCT Median	Program Dashboard	

3. Are our subgroup populations succeeding in this program as well as the overall institution's subgroup populations? Are our subgroup populations succeeding as well as the comparative group? (Success defined as graduation within normal time and employed fulltime in major, within 1 year of graduation)

Metric of Success [KPI]	Program Performance Metric	Benchmark (NA = Not Applicable)	Source/Location	Person Responsible
Stevens' Grant Progression Rate [11B]	5-Year Program Median	5-Year TSCT Stevens' Grant Median & 5-Year Non-Grant Program Median	Program Dashboard	
Stevens' Grant Graduation Rate [11C]	5-Year Program Median	5-Year TSCT Stevens' Grant Median & 5-Year Non-Grant Program Median	Program Dashboard	
% Stevens' Grant Graduates Employed Fulltime in Major (Response Rate) [11D]	5-Year Program Median	5-Year TSCT Median	Program Dashboard	
Minority Progression Rate [12B]	5-Year Program Median	5-Year TSCT Minority Median & 5-Year Non-Minority Program Median	Program Dashboard	

Measure	5-Year Program Median	TSCT Median	Source
Minority Graduation Rate [12C]	5-Year Program Median	5-Year TSCT Minority Median & 5-Year Non-Minority Program Median	Program Dashboard
% Minority Graduates Employed Fulltime in Major (Response Rate) [12D]	5-Year Program Median	5-Year TSCT Median	Program Dashboard
Female Progression Rate [13B]	5-Year Program Median	5-Year TSCT Female Median & 5-Year Non-Female Median	Program Dashboard
Female Graduation Rate [13C]	5-Year Program Median	5-Year TSCT Female Median & 5-Year Non-Female Median	Program Dashboard
% Female Graduates Employed Fulltime in Major (Response Rate) [13D]	5-Year Program Median	5-Year TSCT Median	Program Dashboard
Premajor (in a POS) Progression Rate [12B]	5-Year Program Median	5-Year TSCT Premajor (in a POS) Median & 5-Year Non-Premajor (in a POS) Median	Program Dashboard
Premajor (in a POS) Graduation Rate [12C]	5-Year Program Median	5-Year TSCT Premajor (in a POS) Median & 5-Year Non-Premajor (in a POS) Median	Program Dashboard
% Premajor (in a POS) Employed Fulltime in Major (Response Rate) [12D]	5-Year Program Median	5-Year TSCT Median	Program Dashboard
Athletes, Progression Rate	5-Year Program Median*	5-Year TSCT Athlete Median & 5-Year Non-Athlete Median	Athletics Source Documents & Dashboard
Athletes, Graduation Rate	5-Year Program Median*	5-Year TSCT Athlete Median & 5-Year Non-Athlete Median	Athletics Source Documents & Dashboard
Residency Progression Rate	5-Year Program Median*	5-Year TSCT Resident Median & 5-Year Non-Resident Median	Residence Life Source Documents & Dashboard

	5-Year Program Median*		Source/Location
Residency Graduation Rate	5-Year Program Median*	5-Year TSCT Resident Median & 5-Year Non-Resident Median	Residence Life Source Documents & Dashboard
Students' with Disabilities Progression Rate	5-Year Program Median*	5-Year TSCT Disabilities Median & 5-Year Non-Disabilities Median	Counseling/ Accessibility Source Documents & Dashboard
Students' with Disabilities Graduation Rate	5-Year Program Median*	5-Year TSCT Disabilities Median & 5-Year Non-Disabilities Median	Counseling & Accessibility Source Documents & Dashboard
Act 101 Progression Rate (Students identified as high risk by PA Dept. of Ed.)	5-Year Program Median*	5-Year TSCT ACT 101 Median & 5-Year Non-ACT 101 Median	Act 101 Source Documents & Dashboard
Act 101 Graduation Rate (Students identified as high risk by PA Dept. of Ed.)	5-Year Program Median*	5-Year TSCT ACT 101 Median & 5-Year Non-ACT 101 Median	Act 101 Source Documents & Dashboard

4. Are students, graduates, and employers satisfied with this program?

Metric of Success [KPI]	Program Performance Metric	Benchmark (NA = Not Applicable)	Source/Location	Person Responsible
Student Satisfaction – Quality of Technical Education (Response Rate) [5A]	5-Year Trends*	At or Above 'Good/ Excellent' Rating of 80%	Program Dashboard	
Student Satisfaction – Quality of Technical Education (Response Rate) [5B]	5-Year Trends*	At or Above 'Good/ Excellent' Rating of 80%	Program Dashboard	
Graduate Satisfaction (Response Rate) [7]	5-Year Trends*	TSCT 5-Year Median	Program Dashboard	
Employer Satisfaction "Workforce preparation upon hire" (Response Rate) [9A]	4-Year Aggregate - Rate	At or Above a 'Good/ Very Good' Rating of 80%	Program Dashboard	

	4-Year Aggregate - Rate	At or Above a 'Satisfied/Very Satisfied' Rating of 80%	Program Dashboard	
Employer Satisfaction "Work & Performance Currently within Organization" (Response Rate) [9B]	4-Year Aggregate - Rate	At or Above a 'Satisfied/Very Satisfied' Rating of 80%	Program Dashboard	
Employer Satisfaction "Continue to Hire" (Response Rate) [9C]	4-Year Aggregate - Rate	At or Above a 'Yes' Rating of 80%	Program Dashboard	

5. Are students learning (value added by the institution)?

Metric of Success [KPI]	Program Performance Metric	Benchmark (NA = Not Applicable)	Source/Location	Person Responsible
Technical Education Standardized Assessment - NOCTI or ASE Post-Test Performance	Average Change in Post-to-Pre-Test Total Score Trends*	Evidence of Growth	Program Dashboard	
General Education – Standardized Assessment - ETS Post-Test Performance "Total Score"	Average Change in Post-to-Pre-Test Total Score Trends*	Evidence of Growth	Program Dashboard	
General Education – Standardized Assessment - ETS Post-Test Performance "Critical Thinking"	Average Change in Post-to-Pre-Test Total Score Trends*	Evidence of Growth	Program Dashboard	
General Education – Standardized Assessment - ETS Post-Test Performance "Reading"	Average Change in Post-to-Pre-Test Total Score Trends*	Evidence of Growth	Program Dashboard	
General Education – Standardized Assessment - ETS Post-Test Performance "Writing"	Average Change in Post-to-Pre-Test Total Score Trends*	Evidence of Growth	Program Dashboard	
General Education – Standardized Assessment -	Average Change in Post-to-Pre-Test Total Score Trends*	Evidence of Growth	Program Dashboard	

ETS Post-Test Performance "Mathematics"			
General Education – Standardized Assessment - ETS Post-Test Performance "Humanities"	Average Change in Post-to-Pre-Test Total Score Trends*	Evidence of Growth	Program Dashboard
General Education – Standardized Assessment - ETS Post-Test Performance "Social Sciences"	Average Change in Post-to-Pre-Test Total Score	Evidence of Growth	Program Dashboard
General Education – Standardized Assessment - ETS Post-Test Performance "Natural Sciences"	5-Year Median	At or Above 1 SD of Custom Comparative Mean	Program Dashboard
Employer Satisfaction "Technical Skills" (Response Rate) [9D]	4-Year Aggregate - Rate	At or Above a 'Good/ Very Good' Rating of 80%	Program Dashboard
Employer Satisfaction "Math Skills" (Response Rate) [9E]	4-Year Aggregate - Rate	At or Above a 'Good/ Very Good' Rating of 80%	Program Dashboard
Employer Satisfaction "Reading Skills" (Response Rate) [9F]	4-Year Aggregate - Rate	At or Above a 'Good/ Very Good' Rating of 80%	Program Dashboard
Employer Satisfaction "Writing/Computer Skills" (Response Rate) [9G]	4-Year Aggregate - Rate	At or Above a 'Good/ Very Good' Rating of 80%	Program Dashboard
Employer Satisfaction "Speaking/Listening Skills" (Response Rate) [9H]	4-Year Aggregate - Rate	At or Above a 'Good/ Very Good' Rating of 80%	Program Dashboard
Employer Satisfaction "Critical Thinking/Problem Solving Skills" (Response Rate) [9I]	4-Year Aggregate - Rate	At or Above a 'Good/ Very Good' Rating of 80%	Program Dashboard
Employer Satisfaction "Quality of Work" (Response Rate) [9J]	4-Year Aggregate - Rate	At or Above a 'Good/ Very Good' Rating of 80%	Program Dashboard

	Program Performance Metric	Benchmark	Source/Location	
Employer Satisfaction "Interpersonal Skills" (Response Rate) [9K]	4-Year Aggregate - Rate	At or Above a 'Good/ Very Good' Rating of 80%	Program Dashboard	
Employer Satisfaction "Working Cooperatively with Others" (Response Rate) [9L]	4-Year Aggregate - Rate	At or Above a 'Good/ Very Good' Rating of 80%	Program Dashboard	
Employer Satisfaction "Organizational Skills" (Response Rate) [9M]	4-Year Aggregate - Rate	At or Above a 'Good/ Very Good' Rating of 80%	Program Dashboard	
Employer Satisfaction "Leadership Potential" (Response Rate) [9N]	4-Year Aggregate - Rate	At or Above a 'Good/ Very Good' Rating of 80%	Program Dashboard	
Employer Satisfaction* "Character" (Response Rate) [9O]	4-Year Aggregate - Rate	At or Above a 'Good/ Very Good' Rating of 80%	Program Dashboard	
Employer Satisfaction** "Attitude" (Response Rate) [9P]	4-Year Aggregate - Rate	At or Above a 'Good/ Very Good' Rating of 80%	Program Dashboard	
Employer Satisfaction "Willingness to Learn" (Response Rate) [9Q]	4-Year Aggregate - Rate	At or Above a 'Good/ Very Good' Rating of 80%	Program Dashboard	

6. Is student learning rigorous and consistent with higher education and employer expectations?

Metric of Success [KPI]	Program Performance Metric	Benchmark (NA = Not Applicable)	Source/Location	Person Responsible
Technical Education Standardized Assessment - NOCTI or ASE Post-Test Performance	5-Year Trends	Within or Above 1 SD of National Mean	Program Dashboard	
General Education – Standardized Assessment - ETS Post-Test Performance "Total Score"	5-Year Trends*	Within or Above 1 SD of Custom Comparative Mean	Program Dashboard	
General Education – Standardized Assessment -	5-Year Trends*	Within or Above 1 SD of Custom Comparative Mean	Program Dashboard	

ETS Post-Test Performance "Critical Thinking"	5-Year Trends*	Within or Above 1 SD of Custom Comparative Mean	Program Dashboard
General Education – Standardized Assessment - ETS Post-Test Performance "Reading"	5-Year Trends*	Within or Above 1 SD of Custom Comparative Mean	Program Dashboard
General Education – Standardized Assessment - ETS Post-Test Performance "Writing"	5-Year Trends*	Within or Above 1 SD of Custom Comparative Mean	Program Dashboard
General Education – Standardized Assessment - ETS Post-Test Performance "Mathematics"	5-Year Trends*	Within or Above 1 SD of Custom Comparative Mean	Program Dashboard
General Education – Standardized Assessment - ETS Post-Test Performance "Humanities"	5-Year Trends*	Within or Above 1 SD of Custom Comparative Mean	Program Dashboard
General Education – Standardized Assessment - ETS Post-Test Performance "Social Sciences"	5-Year Trends*	Within or Above 1 SD of Custom Comparative Mean	Program Dashboard
General Education – Standardized Assessment - ETS Post-Test Performance "Natural Sciences"	5-Year Trends*	Within or Above 1 SD of Custom Comparative Mean	Program Dashboard
Employer Satisfaction "Technical Skills" (Response Rate) [9D]	4-Year Aggregate - Rate	At or Above a 'Good/ Very Good' Rating of 80%	Program Dashboard
Employer Satisfaction "Math Skills" (Response Rate) [9E]	4-Year Aggregate - Rate	At or Above a 'Good/ Very Good' Rating of 80%	Program Dashboard
Employer Satisfaction "Reading Skills" (Response Rate) [9F]	4-Year Aggregate - Rate	At or Above a 'Good/ Very Good' Rating of 80%	Program Dashboard

Employer Satisfaction "Writing/Computer Skills" (Response Rate) [9G]	4-Year Aggregate - Rate	At or Above a 'Good/ Very Good' Rating of 80%	Program Dashboard
Employer Satisfaction "Speaking/Listening Skills" (Response Rate) [9H]	4-Year Aggregate - Rate	At or Above a 'Good/ Very Good' Rating of 80%	Program Dashboard
Employer Satisfaction "Critical Thinking/Problem Solving Skills" (Response Rate) [9I]	4-Year Aggregate - Rate	At or Above a 'Good/ Very Good' Rating of 80%	Program Dashboard
Employer Satisfaction "Quality of Work" (Response Rate) [9J]	4-Year Aggregate - Rate	At or Above a 'Good/ Very Good' Rating of 80%	Program Dashboard
Employer Satisfaction "Interpersonal Skills" (Response Rate) [9K]	4-Year Aggregate - Rate	At or Above a 'Good/ Very Good' Rating of 80%	Program Dashboard
Employer Satisfaction "Working Cooperatively with Others" (Response Rate) [9L]	4-Year Aggregate - Rate	At or Above a 'Good/ Very Good' Rating of 80%	Program Dashboard
Employer Satisfaction "Organizational Skills" (Response Rate) [9M]	4-Year Aggregate - Rate	At or Above a 'Good/ Very Good' Rating of 80%	Program Dashboard
Employer Satisfaction "Leadership Potential" (Response Rate) [9N]	4-Year Aggregate - Rate	At or Above a 'Good/ Very Good' Rating of 80%	Program Dashboard
Employer Satisfaction* "Character" (Response Rate) [9O]	4-Year Aggregate - Rate	At or Above a 'Good/ Very Good' Rating of 80%	Program Dashboard
Employer Satisfaction** "Attitude" (Response Rate) [9P]	4-Year Aggregate - Rate	At or Above a 'Good/ Very Good' Rating of 80%	Program Dashboard
Employer Satisfaction "Willingness to Learn" (Response Rate) [9Q]	4-Year Aggregate - Rate	At or Above a 'Good/ Very Good' Rating of 80%	Program Dashboard

*Character is reliability, punctuality, integrity, judgment. maturity, politeness, etc.

43

*Attitude is initiative, cooperation, loyalty, attendance, personal appearance, etc.

7. Are students academically qualified for admission into this program?

Metric	Program Performance Metric	Benchmark (NA = Not Applicable)	Source/Location	Person Responsible
College Success – Reading				
College Success – Writing				
College Success – Mathematics - Algebra				
College Success – Mathematics - Arithmetic				
SAT (Total) or ACT (Composite)				
SAT (Evidence-Based Reading and Writing) or ACT (English)				
SAT or ACT- Mathematics				
ACT - Reading				
ACT - Science				
Transfer Student Transcript Evals				
High School GPA				
HS Attendance				
HS Student Engagement				
Technical Education Standardized Assessment NOCTI/ASE				
Dean of Enrollment Decisions				
Technical Education – Pretest Results (NOCTI or ASE)	Pretest Results for Total and Standard	Within or Above 1 SD of Mean	Scatter Plot Graphs on U-Drive	Program Instructors
General Education Pretest Results (ETS Proficiency Profile) – Total Score, Reading, Critical Thinking,	Pretest Results for Total and Standard	Within or Above 1 SD of Mean	ETS Scaled Score Summary and Roster Report on U-Drive	Program Instructors

| Writing, Mathematics, Natural Science, Social Science, Humanities | | | | |

8. Are students academically engaged in this program?

Metric	Program Performance Metric	Benchmark (NA = Not Applicable)	Source/Location	Person Responsible
SAOS-Student Self-Reflection "Amount of Work Done"	5-Year Program Aggregate Rate for "At Least what was Assigned, if not more"	Meets or Exceeds TSCT Baseline of 94.8%, est. fall 13	Student Academic Opinion Survey (SAOS)	Program Instructors
SAOS-Student Self-Reflection "Well Prepared for Class"	5-Year Program Aggregate Rate for "Most of Time, if not Always"	Meets or Exceeds TSCT Baseline of 94.8%, est. fall 13	Student Academic Opinion Survey (SAOS)	Program Instructors
SAOS-Student Self-Reflection "Assignments Completed & Returned"	5-Year Program Aggregate Rate for "Most of the Time, if not Always"	Meets or Exceeds TSCT Baseline of 93.8%, est. fall 13	Student Academic Opinion Survey (SAOS)	Program Instructors
SAOS-Student Self-Reflection "Asked Questions & Participated in Discussions"	5-Year Program Aggregate Rate for "Most of the Time, if not Always"	Meets or Exceeds TSCT Baseline of 73.4%, est. fall 13	Student Academic Opinion Survey (SAOS)	Program Instructors
SAOS-Student Self-Reflection "Level of Involvement"	5-Year Program Aggregate Rate for "Participated most days or enthusiastic participation"	Meets or Exceeds TSCT Baseline of 79.2%, est. fall 13	Student Academic Opinion Survey (SAOS)	Program Instructors

9. What are student evaluations for this program?

Metric	Program Performance Metric	Benchmark (NA = Not Applicable)	Source/Location	Person Responsible
SAOS-Student Evaluation of Program "Objectives were Clear"	5-Year Program Aggregate Rate for "Agreed or Strongly Agreed"	Meets or Exceeds TSCT Baseline of 84.8%, est. fall 13	Student Academic Opinion Survey (SAOS)	Program Instructors
SAOS-Student Evaluation of Program "Assignments & Exams were Consistent with Syllabus"	5-Year Program Aggregate Rate for "Agreed or Strongly Agreed"	Meets or Exceeds TSCT Baseline of 87.4%, est. fall 13	Student Academic Opinion Survey (SAOS)	Program Instructors

45

Metric	Program Performance Metric	Benchmark (NA = Not Applicable)	Source/Location	Person Responsible
SAOS-Student Evaluation of Program "Practical Knowledge Gained"	5-Year Program Aggregate Rate for "At Least Some if not a Great Deal"	Meets or Exceeds TSCT Baseline of 89.5%, est. fall 13	Student Academic Opinion Survey (SAOS)	Program Instructors
SAOS-Student Evaluation of Program "Reasonable Amount of Reading Required"	5-Year Program Aggregate Rate for "Agreed or Strongly Agreed"	Meets or Exceeds TSCT Baseline of 80.8%, est. fall 13	Student Academic Opinion Survey (SAOS)	Program Instructors
SAOS-Student Evaluation of Program "Reasonable Amount of Writing or Classwork Required"	5-Year Program Aggregate Rate for "Agreed or Strongly Agreed"	Meets or Exceeds TSCT Baseline of 84.3%, est. fall 13	Student Academic Opinion Survey (SAOS)	Program Instructors

10. What are student evaluations for instructors of this program?

Metric	Program Performance Metric	Benchmark (NA = Not Applicable)	Source/Location	Person Responsible
SAOS-Student Evaluation of Instructor "Provided Clear Answers"	5-Year Program Aggregate Rate for "Most of the Time, if not Always"	Meets or Exceeds TSCT Baseline of 81.6%, est. fall 13	Student Academic Opinion Survey (SAOS)	Program Instructors
SAOS-Student Evaluation of Instructor "Encouraged Questions"	5-Year Program Aggregate Rate for "Most of the Time, if not Always"	Meets or Exceeds TSCT Baseline of 84.6%, est. fall 13	Student Academic Opinion Survey (SAOS)	Program Instructors
SAOS-Student Evaluation of Instructor "Considerate"	5-Year Program Aggregate Rate for "Most of the Time, if not Always"	Meets or Exceeds TSCT Baseline of 86.9%, est. fall 13	Student Academic Opinion Survey (SAOS)	Program Instructors
SAOS-Student Evaluation of Instructor "Enthusiastic"	5-Year Program Aggregate Rate for "Most of the Time, if not Always"	Meets or Exceeds TSCT Baseline of 88.5%, est. fall 13	Student Academic Opinion Survey (SAOS)	Program Instructors
SAOS-Student Evaluation of Instructor "Well Organized"	5-Year Program Aggregate Rate for "Most of the Time, if not Always"	Meets or Exceeds TSCT Baseline of 85.4%, est. fall 13	Student Academic Opinion Survey (SAOS)	Program Instructors
SAOS-Student Evaluation of Instructor "Well Prepared for Class on a Daily Basis"	5-Year Program Aggregate Rate for "Most of the Time, if not Always"	Meets or Exceeds TSCT Baseline of 88.1%, est. fall 13	Student Academic Opinion Survey (SAOS)	Program Instructors
SAOS-Student Evaluation of Instructor "Assignments	5-Year Program Aggregate Rate for "Agreed or Strongly Agreed"	Meets or Exceeds TSCT Baseline of 83.5%, est. fall 13	Student Academic Opinion Survey (SAOS)	Program Instructors

Metric	Program Performance Metric	Benchmark	Source/Location	Person Responsible
& Grades Returned in a Reasonable Amount of Time"				
SAOS-Student Evaluation of Instructor "Effectively used Technology and/or Lab Equipment"	5-Year Program Aggregate Rate for "Most of the Time, if not Always"	Meets or Exceeds TSCT Baseline of 81.5%, est. fall 13	Student Academic Opinion Survey (SAOS)	Program Instructors
SAOS-Student Evaluation of Instructor "Effectively Taught Course"	5-Year Program Aggregate Rate for "Most of the Time, if not Always"	Meets or Exceeds TSCT Baseline of 85.9%, est. fall 13	Student Academic Opinion Survey (SAOS)	Program Instructors

11. Are students utilizing support services for this program?

Metric	Program Performance Metric	Benchmark (NA = Not Applicable)	Source/Location	Person Responsible
Peer Tutoring				
Professional Tutoring – Math Lab				
Professional Tutoring – English Lab				
Study Groups				
Student Reported Use of Academic Skills Seminars	Frequency of Use – One or Two, Three to Five, More than Five		ETS Post-Test Questionnaire-Program Folder U Drive	Program Instructors
Student Reported Use of Instructors – During or After Class Hours	Frequency of Use – Practically Every Day, Once A week, Once or Twice	Meets or Exceeds 75% at Least Once, TSCT Baseline, est. Spring '15	ETS Post-Test Questionnaire-Program Folder U Drive	Program Instructors
Follow-up Meeting to Success Navigator				
Counseling Services				
Disability Services				
Test Accommodations				

12. Are at-risk students receiving early alerts in the retention module for this program?

Metric	Program Performance Metric	Benchmark (NA = Not Applicable)	Source/Location	Person Responsible

Academic Early Warning Alerts				
Counseling Early Warning Alerts				
Attendance Early Warning Alerts				
Availability of Student Grades				

13. Are interventions being implemented from the early alerts in the retention module for this program?

Metric	Program Performance Metric	Benchmark (NA = Not Applicable)	Source/Location	Person Responsible
Interventions Implemented				
Responsive Action Communicated				
Attendance 2-Day Warning Letter				
Attendance 5-Day (or more) Dismissal Letter				

14. Are students navigated toward an on-time graduation?

Metric	Program Performance Metric	Benchmark (NA = Not Applicable)	Source/Location	Person Responsible
Model Schedule Observed	Course Sequencing, Success, & Intervention	On-Target to Graduate On-Time	Graduation Report or Course Needs Report	Advisor
Student Reported Advisor contacted them about graduation requirements	At least Once a Semester	100% Aggregate Rate of at "Least Once per Semester"	ETS Post-Test Questionnaire-Program Folder U Drive	Program Instructors
Student Reported Helpfulness of Advisor	Satisfaction of 'Answered my Question' or 'was Very Helpful'	At Least 90% Aggregate of "Answered my Question" or "Was Very Helpful"	ETS Post-Test Questionnaire-Program Folder U Drive	Program Instructors
Course Repeat Trends	Course Grade Trends		Transcripts	Advisors

15. What are the exit reasons for students leaving this program or College prior to Graduation?

48

Metric	Program Performance Metric	Benchmark (NA = Not Applicable)	Source/Location	Person Responsible
Obtained Employment				
Entered Military Service				
Student Illness or Poor Health				
Family Illness or Poor Health				
Death of Student				
Death of Parent				
Marriage				
Childbirth or Childcare				
Financial Difficulty				
Personal Reasons-Describe				
Academic Dismissal				
Academic Difficulty				
Other-Describe				
Transfer				
Dissatisfied with POS				
Unsure/Change of Career Goals				
Residence Life Issues				
Legal Reasons				
Change of Major				
Withdrew				
Academic (A)				
Absenteeism Dismissal (AD)				
Administrative Withdrawal (AW)				
Did Not Meet Grad Requirements (DG)				
Financial (F)				
Moving (M)				
Other (O)				
Transfer to Complete (T)				
Transfer not Completing (X)				

16. What are the Grade Distribution Patterns per Course within the Model Schedule for each POS?

Metric (sample will change with each POS)	Program Performance Metric	Benchmark (NA = Not Applicable)	Source/Location	Person Responsible
Technical Course	D, F, I, W, WF, WP, WS	5-Year Trend Analysis	Jenzebar Grade Distribution by Institutional Division	
Technical Course	D, F, I, W, WF, WP, WS	5-Year Trend Analysis	Jenzebar Grade Distribution by Institutional Division	
Technical Course	D, F, I, W, WF, WP, WS	5-Year Trend Analysis	Jenzebar Grade Distribution by Institutional Division	
Technical Course	D, F, I, W, WF, WP, WS	5-Year Trend Analysis	Jenzebar Grade Distribution by Institutional Division	
Technical Course	D, F, I, W, WF, WP, WS	5-Year Trend Analysis	Jenzebar Grade Distribution by Institutional Division	
Technical Course	D, F, I, W, WF, WP, WS	5-Year Trend Analysis	Jenzebar Grade Distribution by Institutional Division	
Technical Course	D, F, I, W, WF, WP, WS	5-Year Trend Analysis	Jenzebar Grade Distribution by Institutional Division	
Technical Course	D, F, I, W, WF, WP, WS	5-Year Trend Analysis	Jenzebar Grade Distribution by Institutional Division	
Technical Course	D, F, I, W, WF, WP, WS	5-Year Trend Analysis	Jenzebar Grade Distribution by Institutional Division	
Technical Course	D, F, I, W, WF, WP, WS	5-Year Trend Analysis	Jenzebar Grade Distribution by Institutional Division	
Technical Course	D, F, I, W, WF, WP, WS	5-Year Trend Analysis	Jenzebar Grade Distribution by Institutional Division	
Technical Course	D, F, I, W, WF, WP, WS	5-Year Trend Analysis	Jenzebar Grade Distribution by Institutional Division	
MATH 137 Intermediate Alg	D, F, I, W, WF, WP, WS	5-Year Trend Analysis	Jenzebar Grade Distribution by Institutional Division	
MATH 207 PreCalc	D, F, I, W, WF, WP, WS	5-Year Trend Analysis	Jenzebar Grade Distribution by Institutional Division	
MATH 141 Trig	D, F, I, W, WF, WP, WS	5-Year Trend Analysis	Jenzebar Grade Distribution by Institutional Division	
ENG 106	D, F, I, W, WF, WP, WS	5-Year Trend Analysis	Develop Jenzabar Report by POS	

ENG 216	D, F, I, W, WF, WP, WS	5-Year Trend Analysis	Develop Jenzabar Report by POS
PHYS 213	D, F, I, W, WF, WP, WS	5-Year Trend Analysis	Develop Jenzabar Report by POS
Humanities ELEC	D, F, I, W, WF, WP, WS	5-Year Trend Analysis	Develop Jenzabar Report??
General Education ELEC	D, F, I, W, WF, WP, WS	5-Year Trend Analysis	Develop Jenzabar Report??
General Education ELEC	D, F, I, W, WF, WP, WS	5-Year Trend Analysis	Develop Jenzabar Report??
General Education ELEC (if PreCalc)	D, F, I, W, WF, WP, WS	5-Year Trend Analysis	Develop Jenzabar Report??

This structured data driven dialog sheet was developed by the Director of Assessment and Accountability. It was filled in with the data for each program in advance of meetings of the Assessment Committee. This committee consisted of the following individuals: VP Academic Affairs; VP Student Services; VP Finance & Administration; College President; Director of Assessment; Registrar; Dean Enrollment Services; Director and Staff of the Academic Center; Director of Counseling; Director of Residence Life; Faculty of the Program; Program Advisors; Director of Diversity, Inclusion & Equity; Director of Career Services; Director of Athletics; and Director of Financial Aid.

Once the structured data driven dialog sheet is completed it is disseminated to all the members of the Assessment Committee, well in advance. The Assessment Committee then convenes meetings with all of the program's faculty and advisors who were also provided the data driven dialog sheet in advance. The next chapter will explain how this process works to improve a program's performance and, consequently, improve the College's overall performance and fulfillment of its mission.

CHAPTER 4
ACTING ON THE DATA THROUGH CONTINUOUS IMPROVEMENT

In terms of time and effort, by far the most difficult part of the process is identifying, creating, collecting, and presenting the data. Once this is completed, we have actual performance data for each KPI and are in a position to act on this data to improve performance. A good place to begin is with individual program performance using the Data Driven Dialog sheet illustrated in the last chapter. This process consists of comparing a program's KPI to the college's overall KPI for a particular outcome, such as graduation rate. If the college's overall graduation rate is 90 percent and a particular program's graduation rate is 80 percent, it is lowering the college's overall performance and diminishing fulfillment of its mission. Likewise, if a program's graduation rate is 95 percent, it is positively affecting the college's overall graduation rate. In both cases it is important to find the root cause that accounts for the difference in performance. In the case of negative performance, interventions should be implemented to correct the low performance. In the case of positive performance, the root cause, once identified, should be standardized across all programs to improve overall college performance.

The process begins with the Assessment Committee and program's faculty and advisors being provided a Data Driven Dialog Sheet for the program under review. Performance that is three standard deviations above or below the College's median performance is highlighted and the focus of the meetings. After everyone involved has disclosed their preconceived ideas and predictions about the causes for each highlighted KPI, roundtable discussions regarding each KPI are conducted. The goal of each discussion is to determine the root cause of the outcome under discussion. Once the root cause has been agreed upon by the majority, the faculty are tasked with developing a plan to correct performance outcomes that are below the College's median performance or benchmark. Once the

Assessment Committee approves the plan, it is implemented, and the results are reviewed after an agreed upon period of time. An example of how this worked was the College's Electronics Engineering Technology program. This program had an excellent graduate placement rate and above average starting salaries with high graduate and employer satisfaction survey results. However, it had a very low progression rate from the first to the second year which resulted in a low graduation rate. The faculty and advisors of the program were convinced that the problem was that the students entering the program were not academically qualified. However, the data showed that the students admitted to the program were academically qualified and equivalent to students admitted to programs of similar academic rigor, which had much higher progression and graduation rates. After much discussion and research, it was determined that the root cause of the problem was the difficult tests given to students in the first three weeks of the program, which had high failure rates and discouraged students, destroyed their confidence, and led to them dropping out. Another similar program with the College's highest progression and graduation rates took a different approach by moving through the content slower at the beginning and providing special group study sessions in the evenings. These two strategies were incorporated into the Electronics program and resulted in much higher progression and graduation rates.

This process is iterative and applied to all programs and departments of the College; it is continuous. The process that was just described is not occurring at any other college or university in America. The essential aspect of this continuous improvement process is identifying the Key Performance Indicators derived directly from the mission and establishing data collection systems to provide consistent, reliable data over time. There is a phrase in industry called "Management by Walking Around." Simply put, it means that if employees are aware their performance is being observed, it will improve prior to any other intervention. This is the case with the system just described. Faculty are often not even aware that women or minorities are not progressing at the same rate as Caucasian males and if they do, they know that no one is holding them accountable for this disparity. From my perspective as President, it was impossible to monitor and act on performance without reliable information. Dashboards provide the simplest way to achieve this. However, with over a thousand KPI's the task is still difficult. To simplify it, I had performance that was three standard deviations above or below the benchmark, indicated with a red flag for poor performance and a green flag for above average performance. Red flags received attention first, especially if they were a KPI crucial to the College's mission such as graduation rate. An example of this is shown on the next page for critical program KPI's.

Performance Cohorts '11 through '16

PROGRAM	2A: 5yr Median Progression Rate [Avg Perf: 5yr Med within ±5% TSCT 10yr med, 71.0%]	2B: 5yr Median Graduation Rate [Avg Perf: 5yr Med within ±5% TSCT 10yr med, 59.8%]	3: NOCTI, ASE, & PA-DEP Standardized Assessment Results–Technical Education [Avg Perf: 5yr Med within 1 SD National Norms]	4: ETS Standardized Assessment Results–Gen Ed [Avg Perf: 3yr Med within 1 SD of Custom Comparative Group Norms, 5yr Med]	5A: Student Technical Education Quality Rating [Average Performance: Excellent/Good 80-89%]	5B: Student General Education Quality Rating [Average Performance: Excellent/Good 80-89%]	7: Graduate Satisfaction [Average Performance: 5yr Median 4.0]	9: Employer Satisfaction - Workforce Prep [Average Performance: Very Good/Good 80-89%]	11B: 5yr Median Stevens' Grant Prog Rate [Avg Perf ±3% TSCT Stevens' Grant 5yr med, 66.8%]	11C: 5yr Median Stevens' Grant Grad Rate [Avg Perf ±3% TSCT Stevens' Grant 5yr med, 66.4%]	12B: 5yr Median Minority Progression Rate [Avg Performance ±3% TSCT Minority 5yr med, 58.4%]	12C: 5yr Median Minority Graduation Rate [Avg Performance ±3% TSCT Minority 5yr med, 48.9%]	13B: 5yr Median Female Progression Rate [Avg Performance ±3% TSCT Female 5yr med, 70.3%]	13C: 5yr Median Female Graduation Rate [Avg Performance ±3% TSCT Female 5yr med, 59.5%]	14B: 5yr Median Premajor in a POS Prog Rate [Avg Performance ±3% TSCT Premajor 5yr med, 65.2%]	14C: 5yr Median Premajor in a POS Grad Rate [Average Perf ±3% TSCT Premajor 5yr med, 55.2%]
ARCH	0	0	0	0*	+1**	-1**	0	0*	+1	+1	0	+1	-1	-1	0	0
AUTO	0	0	+1	0*	+1**	-1**	+1	-1*	-1	-1	+1	0			+1	0
BUAD-Day	-1	-1	0	0*	-1*	0**	0	-1*	-1	-1	-1	-1	-1*	-1*	0	-1
CABM	0	+1	0	+1*	+1**	-1**	+1	+1*	-1	0					0	+1
CARP	+1	+1	0	0/-1*	+1**	-1**	0	0*	+1	+1	0	-1			+1	+1
CNSA-Day	0	0	0	+1*	+1**	-1**	+1	+1*	+1	+1	+1	0			-1	-1
CNSA-Eve	x	x	0**	x	x	x	x	x	x	x	x	x	x	x	x	x
COEL	+1	+1	0*	-1*	+1**	+1**	0	-1*	+1	-1	0	-1			+1	+1
CORT	0	0	+1	-1*	+1**	-1**	+1	-1*	+1	+1	+1	+1			0	0
CSET	x	x	x	x	x	x	x	x	x	x	x	x	x	x	x	x
ECADT	0	+1	0	0*	0**	-1**	+1	+1*	-1	-1	+1	-1			0	+1
ELEC-Day	+1	+1	0	0*	+1**	-1**	0	-1*	+1	+1	+1	+1			+1	+1
EET	-1	-1	0	+1*	0**	-1**	+1	0	-1	-1	0	-1			-1	-1
ELME	+1**	+1**	0**	0/+1*	-1**	-1**	x	x	+1**	-1**						
GRPH	+1	+1	0	0*	+1**	-1**	0	-1*	+1	0	+1	-1	+1	+1	0	+1
HVAC-Day	0	+1	0	-1*	+1**	0**	0	-1*	0	+1	+1	0			0	+1
HVAC-Eve	0*	-1*	0*	0*	+1**	0**			-1*	-1*	-1*	0*			+1*	-1*
MACH-Day	0	0	0	+1*	x	x	+1	+1*	-1	0	0*	-1*			-1	-1
MACH-Eve	+1*	+1*	0**	0**	x	x			+1*	+1*					+1*	-1*
MASN	-1	-1	0*	0*	+1**	-1**	0	-1*	-1	-1	0	-1			0	-1
MET	0	-1	0	+1*	+1**	-1**	0	+1*	+1	-1	-1	-1			0	-1
MFWT	+1	0	0*	0/+1*	0**	0**	0	+1*	0	+1					0	+1
PLBG	-1	0	0	+1*	+1**	-1**	0	+1*	-1	-1	+1	+1			-1	0
RMDL	x	x	x	0**	+1**	-1**	x	x	x	x	x	x	x	x	x	x
WLDC	+1**	x	0**	0**	0**	-1**	x	x	x	x	x	x	x	x	x	x
WET	-1**	-1**	0*	0*	0**	-1**	x	x	-1**	-1**			-1**	-1**	-1**	-1**

Scores:
+1 indicates excellent performance; **commendations warranted**
0 indicates average performance **on par** with comparative metric; **meeting expectations**
-1 indicates cautionary poor performance; **needs improvement**
-1 indicates critical concern extremely poor performance; **needs improvement**
ID indicates Insufficient Data (most performance based on less than three students per cycle); **needs improvement**
x indicates not applicable as no data exist

Notes:
* = Performance < 5 yrs
** = Single data set
Avg = Average
Med = Median
Norm = Average = Performance
SD = Standard Deviation

Monitoring and acting on Key Performance Indicators, derived directly from a college's mission, is the best and most important way to ensure institutional effectiveness. If you are not measuring, you cannot manage or lead effectively. The board of trustees is responsible for the performance of the institution. Consequently, it is important to keep them informed of the critical Key Performance Indicators through institutional dashboards that are easy to understand. At TSCT this was accomplished by regular presentations at the monthly board meetings. An example of such a presentation is included in Appendix 1.

While the focus of this book has been student outcomes, KPI's for all aspects of the College were created, which as mentioned previously totaled over 1,000. While it is impossible to physically include them all in this book, some examples are provided below.

FACILITIES:
- Median time from work order request to resolution of the issue
- Number of work requests per week
- Percentage of work requests for the same issue
- Percentage of facility usage by semester, day, evening, and weekend
- Number of findings on safety audits

FINANCE:
- Operating Expenses
- Reserve Funds
- Cost per Student
- Cost per Graduate
- Projected Budget to Actual Budget
- Investment Income
- Debt to Equity Ratio
- Days Payable Outstanding
- Findings on Annual Independent Audit

ADVANCEMENT:
- Total Donations to Date
- In-Kind Donations to Date
- Number of Donors
- Median Donation Per Donor

GRANTS:
- Number of Grant Applications Submitted
- Grant Applications by Source (Foundations, Corporations, Government)
- Percentage of Funded Grant Applications (Win Rate)
- Funding Awarded
- Number & Type of Funder

ALUMNI RELATIONS:
- Percentage of Alumni Attended Events
- Percentage of Alumni Who Used Services
- Alumni Satisfaction with Events Attended
- Percentage of Alumni who Made Donations
- Median Alumni Gift
- Alumni Open & Click Rates on Alumni Website

FOOD SERVICE:
- Ratio of Meals Served to Number of Meals Per Meal Plans
- Number and Nature of Student Complaints
- Health Department Audit Reports
- Student Satisfaction with Main Campus Dining Services
- Student Satisfaction with Auxiliary Dining Services

SECURITY:
- Number of Incidents
- Response time for incident
- Cleary Act Reported Incidents
- Number of Cleary Act Violations

MARKETING/SOCIAL MEDIA:
- Marketing cost per application
- Marketing cost per accepted student
- Student acquisition cost
- Digital marketing ROI
- Social media traffic and conversion rates
- Mobile traffic, leads, and conversion rates

HUMAN RESOURCES:
- Absenteeism
- Turnover rate
- Sick Days
- Grievances
- Diversity of Workforce
- Pay Equity
- Training Per Employee

EPILOG

A college or university's board of trustees is responsible for the performance of the institution. Their number one responsibility is to ensure the institution is fulfilling its mission. Other duties include selection and oversight of the president, approval and monitoring of the budget, strategic planning, setting tuition, room, board and other fees, compliance issues, risk management and numerous other obligations. However, the primary responsibility is fulfillment of the mission. In order to do this board members must have and monitor objective, measurable data on key performance indicators (KPI's) derived directly from the mission. Unfortunately, it is the myriad of other obligations that dominate the time of the board. Couple this with the fact that many boards are composed of 30 or more members who only meet three to six times a year and it becomes apparent that the board's most important role is overlooked. Simply look at college and university board agendas or meeting minutes to confirm this fact. If a board is not regularly reviewing the institution's progression, graduation and placement rates, its median student loan debt, graduate satisfaction, employer satisfaction, value-added, and doing so across all student demographics, it is neglecting its most important function.

It is easier to find out about the numerous amenities a college offers such as dining venues, climbing walls, hot tubs, and housekeeper service than it is to find the graduation rate of students who enter a particular college program. The information they do provide would be more relevant for planning a vacation than to determine the best potential educational outcome for a prospective student. Every student should be ensured safety, plenty of healthy food, a supportive environment focused on their success, and opportunities for physical activity and social interaction. However, as described in the first chapter, the quantity and extent of amenities provided by the majority of colleges and universities far exceeds what is required and, in some cases, contributes to student failure.

Higher education should not be a business. Its bottom line is not profit but rather graduates who are educated citizens, who get jobs in their field at a family sustaining salary, and progress in their careers without incurring crushing student loan debt. The current system does not achieve these outcomes at an acceptable level. This book provides a proven model of how to change this, that is applicable to any higher education institution.

APPENDIX 1

Our Performance

. . .

Thaddeus Stevens College of Technology
Institutional Dashboards: Student Success Outcomes

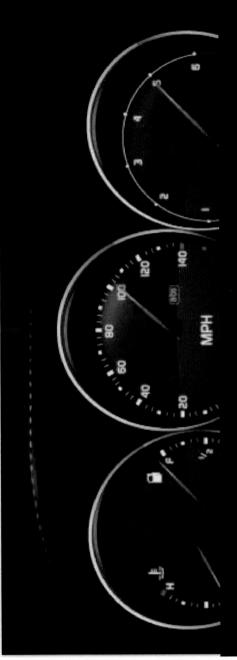

The "institutional dashboard is a management tool that succinctly informs its viewers of the current state of affairs, provides information with which the viewer can evaluate performance, and thereby helps decision-makers strategically move the institution".

(AIR Professional File, Number 123, Institutional Dashboards: Navigational Tool for Colleges and Universities, Page 2)

Institutional Dashboards:
Student Success Outcomes

An overview of performances associated with the institution and derived from data mined during the years 2007 through 2017.

- Readers are encouraged to use the graphical representations as a management tool to support decision making processes at the institution level as well as at the individual program level.

- Key Performance Indicators (KPI) (or student success outcomes) evaluated against the Institutional Policy Outcomes and Mission-Driven Goals ensures the College remains in compliance with its mission, vision, and values.

- Key Performance Indicators contained in the Dashboards support elements of the 7 Strategic Priorities and Accreditation Processes, all of which will guide improvement efforts at the college.

- Identification of strengths and weaknesses further confirms commitment to continuous improvement and learning while at the same time provides assurances that actions align with goals.

Institutional Dashboards: Student Success Outcomes

Consideration should be given to the following:

- At times, outcomes have been calculated on sample sizes that contain fewer than 40 students, so consideration should be exercised when conducting analysis and conclusions. The infrastructure of the college, as well as program design, will continue to cause the occurrence of small sample sizes when disaggregating data by program and/or subgroup. Even so, data-driven decision making is still possible.

- Developing the Dashboards was accomplished through collaboration with the Office of Career Services, Office of Community Service, Office of Financial Aid, Office of Marketing, Administration, Faculty, and other Stakeholders.

- Documenting and analyzing student performance is the first step in making informed decisions and provides further assurance that actions support the mission of Thaddeus Stevens College of Technology. **This is not an end of a process, but rather a beginning.**

Key Performance Indicator 1A:

Our Enrollment ...

Operational Definitions: Enrollment

Official Fall Enrollment (OE): Students enrolled in a credit-bearing course and/or program as of the official fall census date, which is Friday of the second week of semester. Official fall enrollments may include students who are repeating a course, year, or program as well as a student who has changed a major.

Program of Study (POS) Enrollment: Degree seeking students enrolled in a technical program as of the official fall census date.

Freshmen Enrollment: Degree seeking students enrolled in the first year of a POS as of the official fall census date.

Sophomore Enrollment: Degree seeking students enrolled in the second year of a POS as of the official fall census date.

Premajor Enrollment: Students enrolled who require remediation in reading, writing, and/or mathematics. In most cases, college entrance is based on specific admission criteria, whereas the level of and duration of remediation is based on scores earned at the time of placement testing. Remedial programs varied throughout the years and are noted within the graphical representations as T-STEP, APEX, DTP, DEV, or Premajor. To comply with language used by the college, Premajor is used in two contexts: as a descriptor used to reference all students who needed academic remediation as well as to identify a specific remedial program established in Summer '11 and Fall '11. Notation of use in context as to the type of remedial program is noted within the horizontal axis labels of each graphical representation, whereas the overall reference to remediated students is used in the title and for general purposes. Further clarification will be made available to readers where applicable and when necessary. As of 2004, students remediated through a program at the college have been coded in the student information management system (Jenzabar) as PRE. Although students in remedial course are considered 'freshmen', they are not included in the POS counts until matriculation into a POS. Premajor courses are credit-bearing; however, credit hours earned do not tabulate toward graduation credits.

Academics Only: Students enrolled in all general studies courses as of the official fall census date.

Annual Enrollment Growth Rate: The percent of change that the official fall enrollment has gained or loss within a specific period of time and according to a specified context. (Formula: $\frac{\text{current enrollment - previous enrollment}}{\text{previous enrollment}}$ x 100)

71

Official Fall Enrollment

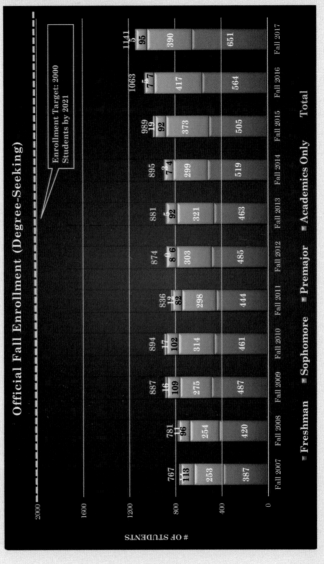

Official Fall Enrollment (Degree-Seeking)

Enrollment Target: 2000 Students by 2021

	Fall 2007	Fall 2008	Fall 2009	Fall 2010	Fall 2011	Fall 2012	Fall 2013	Fall 2014	Fall 2015	Fall 2016	Fall 2017
Total	767	781	887	894	836	874	881	895	989	1063	1141
Freshman	113	96	16	17	12	8	5	7	19	7	5
Sophomore		11	109	102	82	6	92	4	92	7	95
Premajor	253	254	275	314	298	303	321	299	373	417	390
Academics Only	387	420	487	461	444	485	463	519	505	564	651

OF STUDENTS

■ Freshman ■ Sophomore ■ Premajor ■ Academics Only ■ Total

Total enrollment is the sum of the 4 distinct groups previously defined as: Freshmen, Sophomore, Premajor (used in general context) and Academics Only. All are students enrolled at the college in credit-bearing classes or programs at the time of the official fall census report.

Table of Contents

Key Performance Indicator 1B:

Our Enrollment Growth Rates …

Annual Enrollment Growth Rate *(percent of change)*

Year to Year	Fresh (POS)	Soph (POS)	Total (POS)	Fresh (A1 national)	TOTAL
Fall 2004-to-2003	-9.3%	4.8%	-3.3%	na	-0.9%
Fall 2005-to-2004	-14.0%	-4.2%	-9.1%	na	0.9%
Fall 2006-to-2005	6.3%	-8.4%	-0.2%	-3.0%	-1.0%
Fall 2007-to-2006	14.5%	10.5%	12.9%	16.5%	15.0%
Fall 2008-to-2007	8.5%	0.4%	6.3%	15.0%	1.8%
Fall 2009-to-2008	16.0%	8.3%	13.1%	13.5%	13.6%
Fall 2010-to-2009	-0.3%	14.2%	1.7%	-0.4%	0.8%
Fall 2011-to-2010	-3.1%	-5.1%	-4.3%	-19.6%	-6.5%
Fall 2012-to-2011	9.2%	1.1%	6.2%	4.9%	4.5%
Fall 2013-to-2012	-4.8%	5.9%	-0.5%	7.0%	0.8%
Fall 2014-to-2013*	12.1%	-9.9%	4.3%	-19.6%	1.6%
Fall 2015-to-2014**	-4.7%	24.7%	1.3%	24.3%	10.5%
Fall 2016-to-2015	11.7%	11.0%	11.7%	-10.3%	1.5%
Fall 2017-to-2016****	**15.4%**	**-6.5%**	**6.1%**	**23.4%**	**7.3%**
Average Annual Growth Rate	4.0%	3.7%	3.7%	0.8%	4.0%
Median Annual Growth Rate	7.4%	3.2%	4.8%	0.9%	1.7%

A Few Observations Regarding Fall '17-to-Fall '16 Enrollment Growth Rates:

Freshmen (in POS) enrollment experienced an astounding +15.4% growth, which can be attributed to two primary factors:

- Adoption of new program (CSET = +4.3% contribution)

- Filling pre-existing programs to a greater degree of capacity (+11.2% contribution)

Sophomores (in POS) enrollment experienced an -6.5% decline in enrollment. However, of more significance when examining the POS that had sophomore enrollments in fall 2016 and fall 2017, a more substantial decrease is revealed -15.1%, which can be attributed to a lack of retention.

Backed out 36 sophomore students from the fall '17 count [CNSA Eve (14), MACH Eve (9), and WELD (13)]. Percent of change formula: (354-417/417)

Freshmen premajor enrollment experienced a +23.4% increase.

- Overall, the total enrollment growth rate for the College experienced a +7.3% increase. According to the National Student Clearinghouse Research Center (NSCRC), the fall 2017-to-fall 2016 reporting cycle indicated enrollment for two-year public postsecondary Title IV, degree-granting institutions decreased by -9.1% at the national level and by -0.8% at the state level. **In other words, the College's growth is more than 8 times greater than our comparable state metric and 16 times greater than our national metric!** (*Benchmark Source:* http://nscresearchcenter.org; *Report: Current Term Enrollment Estimates Fall 2017, Table 8, p. 11-13*)

Projection: To reach the target enrollment goal of 2000 students in Fall 2021, the average annual rate of growth expected is +12.7% per annual calculation. (Baseline established in Fall 2011 total enrollment was 836 students.) Note: Slight variance in percentage sum due to rounding.

Key Performance Indicator 1C:

Our Enrollment by Subgroup ...

Official Fall Freshmen Enrollment
by Subgroup and Total

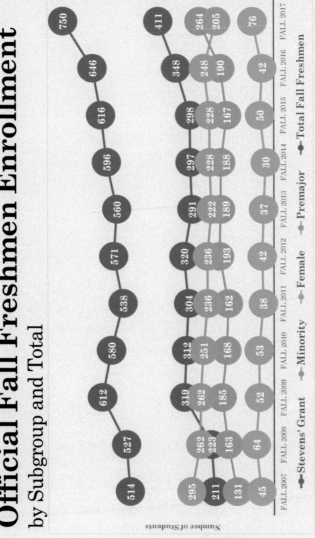

Number of Students

	FALL 2007	FALL 2008	FALL 2009	FALL 2010	FALL 2011	FALL 2012	FALL 2013	FALL 2014	FALL 2015	FALL 2016	FALL 2017
Total Fall Freshmen	514	527	612	580	538	571	560	596	616	646	750
Stevens' Grant	295	262	319	312	304	320	291	297	298	348	411
Minority	211	223	262	251	236	236	222	228	228	248	264
Female	131	163	185	168	162	193	189	188	167	190	205
Premajor	45	64	52	53	38	42	37	30	50	42	76

Stevens' Grant   Minority   Female   Premajor   Total Fall Freshmen

Overall Total Fall Freshmen enrollment is the number of students at the college who were enrolled in credit-bearing courses or programs at the time of the official fall census report. There are 4 distinct subgroups: Stevens' Grant, Minority, Female, and Premajor (used in general context). Premajor counts are inclusive of those in a program of study as well as those in the fall remedial program.

Key Performance Indicator 2:

Our Progression & Graduation Rates ...

Operational Definitions:
Progression & Graduation

Persistence: Term-to-term advancement.
    Persistence Rate: The number of students officially enrolled in the spring semester of the freshmen year divided by the number of students officially enrolled in the fall semester of the freshmen year. Used in the calculation of progression rate for students pursuing a 9-month certificate. Also applicable to calculating the persistence rate within the remedial programs.

Retention: Continuous fall-to-fall advancement.
    Retention Rate: The number of students officially enrolled in the fall semester of the sophomore year divided by the number of students officially enrolled in the fall semester of the freshmen year. Applicable to associate degree programs.

Progression: Successful persistence.
    Progression Rate: Represents the successful term-to-term persistence rate of students pursuing a certificate as well as the continuous fall-to-fall advancement (retention) rate of students pursuing an associate degree.

Graduate: A student who has successfully completed a program of study earning a degree and/or certificate.
    Graduation Rate (Certificate): The number of students earning a certificate in fewer than two consecutive years divided by the number of freshmen students officially enrolled in the fall semester of their freshmen year.
    Graduation Rate (Associate Degree): The number of students earning a degree in fewer than three consecutive years divided by the number of freshmen students officially enrolled in the fall semester of the preceding year.

Progression & Graduation Rates
by Graduating Class

Institutional Rates
10-Yr Median ('08-'17)
ProgR = 71.0%
GradR = 60.7%

—— Progression Rate   —— Graduation Rate (Normal-Time)

	Class 13	Class 14	Class 15	Class 16	Class 17
OE Freshmen	498	522	468	513	543
OE Sophomores	353	371	323	391	452
Progression Rate	70.9%	71.1%	69.0%	76.2%	83.2%
Graduates (Normal-Time)	308	310	271	336	384
Graduation Rate (Normal-Time)	61.8%	59.4%	57.9%	65.5%	70.7%

***Progression Rate** reflects the continuous term-to-term persistence rate for students enrolled in certificate programs and the fall-to-fall retention rate for students enrolled in associate degree programs.*
***Graduation Rate** reflects the number of freshmen who were officially enrolled in the fall semester and earned a certificate or degree within the expected timeframe.*

*Key Performance
Indicator 10A:*

Our Graduate
Placement ...

Operational Definitions: Graduate

<u>Graduate</u>: A student who has earned alumni status with the college.

<u>Graduate Survey</u>: A survey sent to a graduate within the first year of completing a program of study. The survey platform used to collect, store, and analyze the self-reported responses from the graduates is survey monkey.

<u>Response Rate</u>: Percentage of graduates who responded with their employment information.

<u>Placement</u>: Graduates employed full-time or continuing their education on a full-time basis.

    <u>Overall Placement Rate</u>: Percentage of "respondents" who reported being employed full-time or continuing their education on a full-time basis.

    <u>Employed FT or Cont. ED</u>: Percentage of "respondents" who reported being employed full-time in major or continuing their education on a full-time basis.

    <u>Employed FT in Major Rate</u>: Percentage of "respondents" who are employed full-time in their program of study (Major).

    <u>Continuing Education Rate</u>: Percentage of "respondents" who are continuing education on a full-time basis.

<u>Employer/Job Tracking</u>: Number of employers recruiting and jobs available to TSCT students/graduates during a specific graduating class's degree program. Data is pulled via College Central Network, the college's internal job posting website. Employer/Job tracking in this dashboard includes data starting with the class of 2014.

Graduate Survey Response Rate: Overall

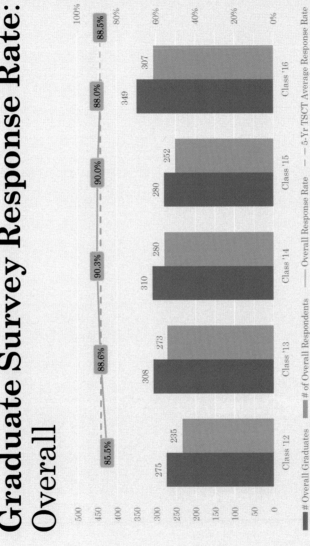

Data and Graph Source: Director of Career Services. A data label of 0% indicates an actual 0%, whereas the absence of a data point and label indicates a null data set.

Graduate Placement Rate:
Overall

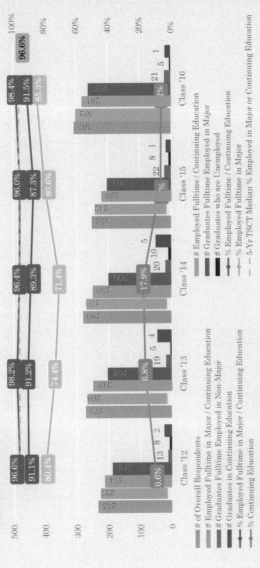

*Key Performance
Indicator 11:*

Our Graduates'
Satisfaction ...

Graduate Satisfaction: Total Population

How well did your program of study prepare you for your current position?

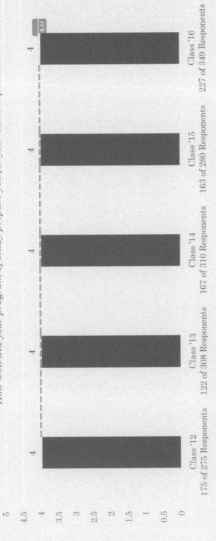

Class '12	Class '13	Class '14	Class '15	Class '16
175 of 275 Respondents	122 of 308 Respondents	167 of 310 Respondents	163 of 280 Respondents	227 of 349 Respondents

— Median Overall Rating per Year   – – 5-Year TSCT Median Overall Satisfaction

The responses are evaluated on a 5-point Likert scale:

5- Excellent   4-Good   3-Adequate   2-Inadequate   1-Not at all

*Student satisfaction is based on the graduate survey response to the question, "How well did your program of study prepare you for your current position?" The responses are evaluated on a 5-point Likert scale. *Medians are based on responses received. Data and Graph Source: Director of Career Services.*

85

Key Performance Indicator 12:

Our Graduates' Starting Salary ...

Graduate Survey:
Annual Starting Salary

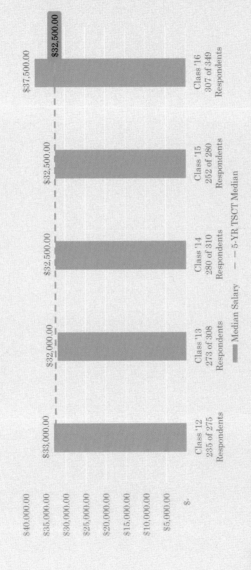

$40,000.00				
$35,000.00	$33,000.00	$32,000.00	$32,500.00	$32,500.00	$37,500.00
$30,000.00				
$25,000.00				
$20,000.00				
$15,000.00				
$10,000.00				
$5,000.00				
$-				

Class '12   Class '13   Class '14   Class 15   Class '16
235 of 275   273 of 308   280 of 310   252 of 280   307 of 349
Respondents   Respondents   Respondents   Respondents   Respondents

$32,500.00

— Median Salary   - - - 5-YR TSCT Median

Annual Starting Salary is based on the graduate survey response to the request to identify a starting salary from a range of options. This graph shows the median first year annual salary. All calculations are based on the respondent's self-reported first year annual income. Data and Graph Source: Director of Career Services.

Table of Contents

*Key Performance
Indicator 13:*

Our Employers’
Satisfaction …

Employer Survey:
Overall Employer Satisfaction

120%

100%

80%

60%

40%

20%

0%

| 86% | 98% | 98% |

44.39%

How would you rate TSCT Graduates in their overall workforce preparation UPON HIRE? Graph Indicates "Very Good or Good".

How would you rate your level of satisfaction with the work and performance of TSCT graduates CURRENTLY WITHIN your organization? Graph indicates "Very Satisfied or Satisfied".

Will you continue to hire TSCT students and graduates? Graph indicates "Yes".

— % Employer Respondents (218 of 491)

Employer satisfaction is based on the responses collected through an on-line survey distributed to employers of Stevens' graduates. Graph represents combined responses of employers of graduates from classes '13, '14, '15, '16. Employers responded to the questions regarding their satisfaction of Thaddeus Stevens College of Technology Graduates' level of preparation upon hire and performance on the job. Responses are evaluated on a Likert scale. Data and Graph Source: Director of Career Services.

89

Key Performance Indicator 14:

Our Graduates' Loan Debt ...

Percent of Graduates with Loan Debt & Amount of Student Debt

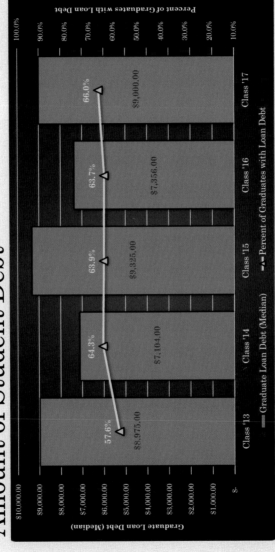

Student Loan Profile is derived from combining the total amount of all student loans received by the student during their time at Stevens. (Since TSCT is a residential college, much of the debt is incurred as a result of room and board expenses.)
- *Graduates with Loan Debt reflects the percentage of students with loan debt.*
- *Graduate Loan Debt indicates the median amount of student loan debt.*

Data Source: Director of Financial Aid

91

Thaddeus Stevens College of Technology

Subgroup Dashboards:
Stevens' Grant, Minority, Female, and Premajor in POS

Official Fall Enrollments of 2010 – 2016
Graduating Classes of 2012 – 2016
Post-Graduate Classes of 2011 – 2015

Subgroup:

Stevens' Grant

The group of students who received college-level funding based on a specific set of financial conditions. The subgroup is comprised of Stevens' Grant, Legacy, and Grant Suspended. The comparative group includes all others who do not meet the subgroup criteria. Since Stevens grant recipients sometimes vary from semester to semester or year to year, there are times when progression and graduation rates may exceed 100%, indicating a greater number of students qualified for a grant in the concluding cohort than the freshmen cohort. This occurrence provides pertinent information regarding the financial stability of our student body.

*Key Performance
Indicator 16A:*

Our Stevens' Grant
Enrollment ...

Stevens' Grant Enrollment in Proportion to Official Fall Freshmen Enrollment

Stevens' Grant in Comparison with Non-Stevens' Grant

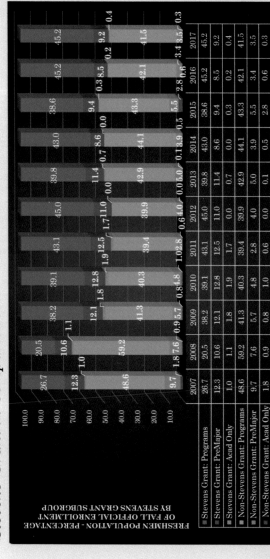

FRESHMEN POPULATION - PERCENTAGE OF FALL OFFICIAL ENROLLMENT BY STEVENS GRANT SUBGROUP

	2007	2008	2009	2010	2011	2012	2013	2014	2015	2016	2017
Stevens Grant: Programs	26.7	20.5	38.2	39.1	43.1	45.0	39.8	43.0	38.6	45.2	45.2
Stevens Grant: PreMajor	12.3	10.6	12.1	12.8	12.5	11.0	11.4	8.6	9.4	8.5	9.2
Stevens Grant: Acad Only	1.0	1.1	1.8	1.9	1.7	0.0	0.7	0.0	0.3	0.2	0.4
Non-Stevens Grant: Programs	48.6	59.2	41.3	40.3	39.4	39.9	42.9	44.1	43.3	42.1	41.5
Non-Stevens Grant: PreMajor	9.7	7.6	5.7	4.8	2.8	4.0	5.0	3.9	5.5	3.4	3.5
Non-Stevens Grant: Acad Only	1.8	0.9	0.8	1.0	0.6	0.1	0.1	0.5	2.8	0.6	0.3

Stevens' Grant Enrollment in Proportion to Official Fall Freshmen Enrollment is based on the number of officially enrolled fall Stevens' Grant freshmen divided by the total official fall freshmen enrollment. The sum of all groups is 100% of the total official fall freshmen enrollment, with slight variations because of rounding.

Table of Contents

*Key Performance
Indicator 16B:*

Our Stevens' Grant Progression Rate ...

Stevens' Grant Progression Rate
In Comparison with Other & 5-Year Median

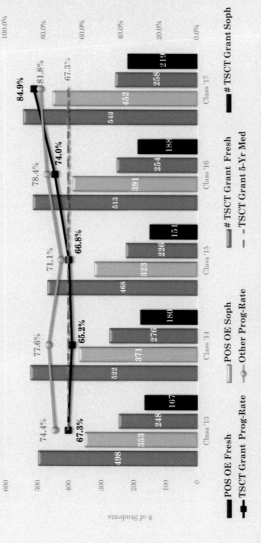

Progression rate reflects the continuous term-to-term persistence rate for students enrolled in certificate programs and the fall-to-fall retention rate for students enrolled in associate degree programs. Graph reflects official fall POS enrollments for freshmen, sophomore, Stevens' Grant freshmen, and Stevens' Grant sophomore. Key Performance Indicators: Progression Rate of Stevens' Grant to Progression Rate of "Other", Progression Rate of Stevens' Grant to 5-Year Median Stevens' Grant Progression Rate, and Performance Gap between the two comparative groups.

97

Key Performance
Indicator 16C:

Our Stevens' Grant
Graduation Rate …

Stevens' Grant Graduation Rate
In Comparison with Other & 5-Year Median
Within Normal-Time

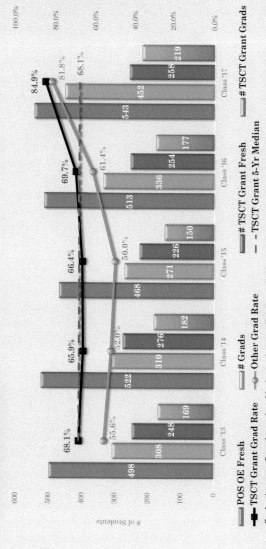

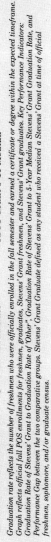

Graduation rate reflects the number of freshmen who were officially enrolled in the fall semester and earned a certificate or degree within the expected timeframe. Graph reflects official fall POS enrollments for freshmen, graduates, Stevens' Grant freshmen, and Stevens' Grant graduates. Key Performance Indicators: Graduation Rate of Stevens' Grant to Graduation Rate of "Other", Graduation Rate of Stevens' Grant to 5-Year Median Stevens' Grant Graduation Rate, and Performance Gap between the two comparative groups. Stevens' Grant Graduate defined as any student who received a Stevens' Grant at time of official freshmen, sophomore, and/or graduate census.

*Key Performance
Indicator 16D:*

Our Stevens' Grant
Graduate Placement ...

Graduate Survey:
Stevens' Grant Response Rate

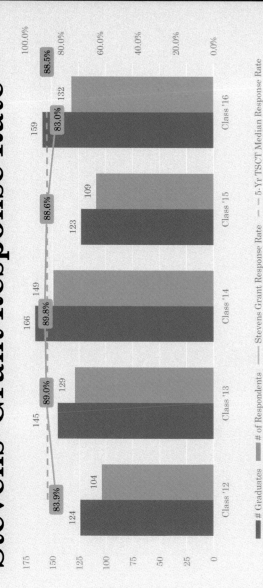

Data Line Graph Source: Office of Career Services. A data label of 0% indicates an actual 0%, whereas the absence of a data point and

Graduate Survey:
Stevens' Grant Placement Rate

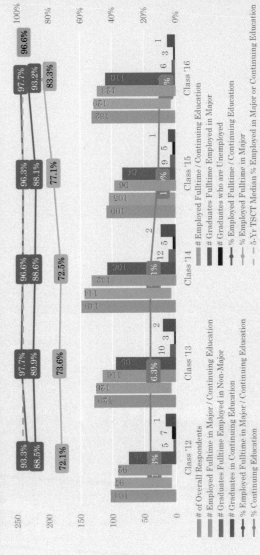

# of Overall Respondents
Employed Fulltime in Major / Continuing Education
Graduates Fulltime Employed in Non-Major
Graduates in Continuing Education
% Employed Fulltime in Major / Continuing Education
% Continuing Education

Employed Fulltime / Continuing Education
Graduates Fulltime Employed in Major
Graduates who are Unemployed
% Employed Fulltime / Continuing Education
% Employed Fulltime in Major
5-Yr TSCT Median % Employed in Major or Continuing Education

Placement Rates for Stevens' Grant Population.
Placement Rate: Percentage of "respondents" who reported being employed full-time or continuing their education on a full-time basis (green line).
Employment within Field Rate: Percentage of "respondents" who are employed full-time in their field of study (blue line).
Unemployment Rate 5 Year Median: 3.2% - 36 out of 1347 Respondents
Data and Graph Source: Director of Career Services. A data label of 0% indicates an actual 0%, whereas the absence of a data point and label indicates a null data set.

102

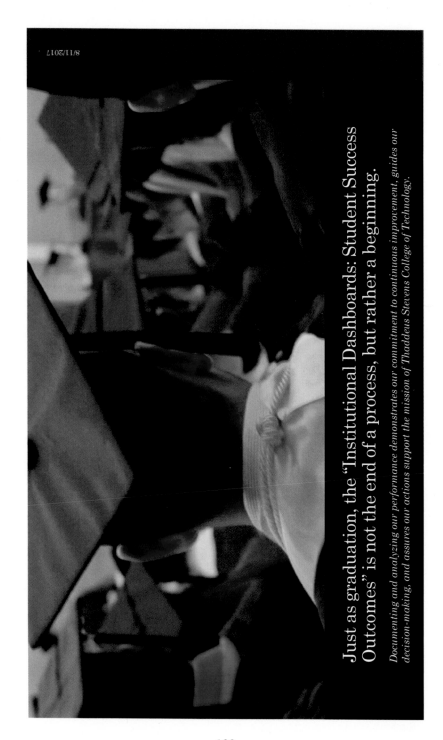

Just as graduation, the "Institutional Dashboards: Student Success Outcomes" is not the end of a process, but rather a beginning.

Documenting and analyzing our performance demonstrates our commitment to continuous improvement, guides our decision-making, and assures our actions support the mission of Thaddeus Stevens College of Technology.

APPENDIX 2

August 1, 2019

Dear President William Griscom:

I am deeply concerned by recent student protests at Swarthmore College that indicate how much work remains to ensure that every student has a safe learning environment. As the author of the Campus SaVE Act, which was enacted as a part of the Violence Against Women Reauthorization Act of 2013 (also referred to as the "VAWA Amendments to the Clery Act"),[1] I have worked to ensure rigorous protections against sexual assault, dating violence, domestic violence and stalking for students, and to create appropriate guardrails to ensure that colleges and universities are taking action to protect all students. Institutions of higher education need to be places where students can learn and grow without fear. That means that school administrators need to work with students to create a culture of safety and accountability, through ongoing efforts and not just in response to a crisis.

As you know, under the Campus SaVE Act, all institutions must have in place policies and programs to prevent sexual violence; to ensure victims of sexual violence understand their rights and the resources available to them; and to ensure prompt, fair and impartial disciplinary action. I urge you to review Thaddeus Stevens College of Technology's policies and practices to ensure that you are in full compliance with the law, and that you are working with students to create a safe and welcoming environment for all students that

---

[1] The Campus SaVE Act has now been in effect for four academic years.